REDISCOVER THE FINAL FRONTIER.

Set ten years prior to the *U.S.S. Enterprise* embarking on her
historic five-year mission, *Star Trek: Discovery* takes place
during a period of galactic turmoil.

At the edge of known space, the *U.S.S. Shenzhou* encounters an ancient
Klingon object, and her first officer, Michael Burnham, crosses a line.
As conflict erupts between the United Federation of Planets and the Klingon
Empire, and chaos sweeps across the Galaxy, can the Federation's ideals
of equality and peaceful co-existence survive?
And can Burnham, with the new crew of the *U.S.S. Discovery*,
help end this war that she started?

TITAN EDITORIAL
Editor **Christopher Cooper**
Senior Editor **Martin Eden**
Editorial Assistant **Tolly Maggs**
Senior Production Controller
Maria Pearson
Production Controller **Jackie Flook**
Production Controller **Peter James**
Art Director **Oz Browne**
Senior Sales Manager **Steve Tothill**

Subscriptions Executive **Tony Ho**
Direct Sales & Marketing Manager
Ricky Claydon
Brand Manager, Marketing
Lucy Ripper
Advertising Assistant **Tom Miller**
Commercial Manager
Michelle Fairlamb
U.S. Advertising Manager **Jeni Smith**
Publishing Manager **Darryl Tothill**

Publishing Director **Chris Teather**
Operations Director **Leigh Baulch**
Executive Director **Vivian Cheung**
Publisher **Nick Landau**

CONTRIBUTORS:
Kristin Baver
Chris Gardner
Ian Spelling
Karen Stoddard Hayes

DISTRIBUTION
US Newsstand: Total Publisher Services, Inc.
John Dziewiatko wski, 630-851-7683
US Distribution: Source Interlink, Curtis Circulation
Company
UK Newsstand: Marketforce, 0203 7879199
US/UK Direct Sales Market: Diamond
Comic Distributors

For more info on advertising contact
adinfo@titanemail.com

Star Trek: Discovery The Official Collector's Edition
is published by Titan Magazines, a division of Titan
Publishing Group Limited, 144 Southwark Street, London
SE1 0UP. For sale in the US, Canada, UK and Eire
ISBN: 9781785861574

CONTENTS

VOYAGE OF DISCOVERY

IT'S BEEN A LONG ROAD

Star Trek: Discovery's two-year journey from concept to screen has not been without its dramas, twists, and revelations, but the end result is a new vision of *Star Trek* that respects the original while reaching towards dramatic new frontiers.

Words: Ian Spelling

On May 13, 2005, as the end credits rolled on the final episode of *Star Trek: Enterprise*, it looked as if we'd reached the outer limits of the final frontier.

Despite a late burst of creative energy, the series had suffered in the ratings, and barely secured a fourth season before network UPN pulled the plug. The series finale, "These Are the Voyages…," was intended as a love letter to a remarkable 18-year *Trek* television renaissance that encompassed each of the sequels to the original *Star Trek* series: *The Next Generation, Deep Space Nine, Voyager,* and *Enterprise.* Sadly, it did so in underwhelming fashion, and with *Star Trek Nemesis* having already ended *Trek's* run of cinematic outings, the franchise seemed to have reached the end of the road.

"On November 2, 2015, CBS Television Studios announced that it was developing a totally new *Star Trek* television series."

Star Trek remained in stasis until 2009, when producer-director J.J. Abrams and his Bad Robot team scored a box office hit with their big-screen reboot. *Star Trek (2009)* wowed audiences, and was followed by two sequels – *Star Trek Into Darkness,* and *Star Trek Beyond* – with talk of a fourth outing in the pipeline. The

trio of movies played well across the globe, revitalizing the franchise, and increasing the public's demand for a fresh *Star Trek* TV series.

Still, it was a big surprise, even to those in-the-know, when on November 2, 2015, CBS Television Studios announced that it was developing a totally new *Star Trek* television series – only, not for television.

NEW FRONTIERS

Since *Star Trek* last graced TV screens, the media landscape has changed incredibly. Traditional network television has seen a huge slice of the broadcasting pie taken by on-demand, streaming content providers like Netflix, Hulu, and Amazon, and CBS decided to move with the times. Launching their own streaming

02

01 *Discovery* cast grab a selfie at San Diego Comic-Con: Jason Isaacs, Mary Wiseman, Anthony Rapp, James Frain, Doug Jones, Shazad Latif, and Sonequa Martin-Green.

02 The incredible bridge set for the Klingon sarcophagus ship, under construction at Pinewood Studios, Toronto.

platform, CBS All Access, this would be the home of the new *Star Trek*, with the as-yet-untitled show being distributed around the world by CBS Studios International.

At this point, the new *Trek* didn't have a premise, or even a showrunner. For fans, it was enough to know that their show was coming back – which was a good job, as they would have to wait another three months for any further news.

On February 9, 2016, and much to the delight of fans, CBS Television Studios announced that Bryan Fuller was on board to co-create and co-executive produce the new *Trek* series (with Alex Kurtzman, co-writer of the first two Bad Robot movies). Fuller, the writer-producer of hit shows including *Wonderfalls, Pushing Daisies,* and *Hannibal,* is a lifelong *Trek* fan, who'd cut his teeth on the writing staffs of both *Deep Space Nine* and *Voyager.* As showrunner, Fuller immediately dived into the nitty-gritty of creating and mounting the new show, defining its central theme and overseeing the design and casting process.

Another link to the past was revealed a few weeks later, when it was announced that Nicholas Meyer (co-writer and director of *Star Trek II: The Wrath of Khan,* and *Star Trek VI: The Undiscovered Country,* as well as co-writer of *Star Trek IV: The Voyage Home*), had joined the writing staff.

> ## "I COULDN'T THINK OF A MORE *STAR TREK*-THEMED NAME FOR A SHIP THAN *DISCOVERY.*"
> ### BRYAN FULLER

May brought fans their first taste of the series, with a very brief teaser for the show (little more than a redesigned Starfleet emblem), and the news that it would start filming in Toronto, Canada, in the fall of 2016.

While US fans already knew where they would be getting their fix of *Star Trek,* internationally the picture had remained vague until CBS Studios International revealed that the new series would be broadcast exclusively by Bell Media in Canada and Netflix in the rest of the world.

NAMING THE SHIP

As *Star Trek* began a year-long celebration of its 50th anniversary, Bryan Fuller hosted a special panel at San Diego Comic-Con, on July 23, 2016. It was there that he revealed the title of the new series, and the name of its lead ship: *Discovery.*

"There are so many reasons why we settled on *Discovery,*" Fuller told

startrek.com about choosing the name. "But the chief one amongst them was that I couldn't think of a more *Star Trek*-themed name for a ship than *Discovery.*"

Fans were also treated to a short promo showing the full *Star Trek: Discovery* logo, and what Fuller described as footage of the *U.S.S. Discovery*'s "test flight" – an early concept animation of the ship, specially prepared for the Comic-Con panel.

More information was released during August, answering some big questions that had been causing a stir on *Trek* forums: When would *Discovery* be set, and would it take place in the Prime universe of its predecessors, or in the *Kelvin* timeline of the Bad Robot movies? Fuller revealed that *Discovery* would be 13 episodes long, and take place ten years before the original *Star Trek.* It would feature a woman as the central character, although she would not be the ship's captain, and the crew would include a gay character as a series regular for the first time.

Then came the first bump in the road. On September 24, CBS All Access announced that it had shifted the show's debut to May 2017.

Executive producers Kurtzman and Fuller released a joint statement that read, "Bringing *Star Trek* back to television carries a responsibility

03

and mission: to connect fans and newcomers alike to the series that has fed our imaginations since childhood. We aim to dream big and deliver, and that means making sure the demands of physical and post-production for a show that takes place entirely in space, and the need to meet an air date, don't result in compromised quality. Before heading into production, we evaluated these realities with our partners at CBS and they agreed: *Star Trek* deserves the very best, and these extra few months will help us achieve a vision we can all be proud of."

CHANGE AT THE HELM

A little over a month later, CBS Television Studios released a statement confirming that Fuller had stepped aside as showrunner, although he'd retain an executive producer credit. Already committed to producing another show, *American Gods*, Fuller had decided to focus on that series, so his longtime associates Gretchen Berg and Aaron Harberts came aboard as the new showrunners, joining Kurtzman in overseeing production of *Discovery*.

Time marched on, and the series was still very much in pre-production as we moved into 2017. However, the cast was beginning to take shape, with some big names securing high-ranking roles, including Michelle Yeoh as Captain Georgiou, and Jason Isaacs as Captain Lorca. Two captains, but as

yet no Number One – the first officer that would be the central player in the series. Rumors persisted that a member of *The Walking Dead* cast would be filling that role, but no official news was forthcoming from CBS. Fans would have to wait until later in the year for confirmation, but first they would have to deal with another blow as, in January 2017, CBS All Access announced that *Discovery* would no longer premiere in May. A new launch date was not given, although it was confirmed that production was now fully underway.

Come April 3rd, 2017, the worst-kept secret in Hollywood was let out of the bag, when Sonequa Martin-Green was finally confirmed as *Discovery*'s lead. CBS had been contractually obliged to keep her casting secret until after *The Walking Dead* aired its season 7 finale, in which Martin-Green's character in the show, Sasha Williams, met her grizzly end.

DISCOVERING DISCOVERY

May brought another welcome revelation – an additional two episodes had been added to *Discovery*'s first season run – and fans were treated to the series' first trailer, giving them a long-awaited glimpse of Martin-Green as Michael Burnham, and the series' new-look Klingons.

The biggest news yet came the following month – *Discovery*'s launch date. The series would debut in the US on September 24, 2017, and on Netflix internationally on the 25th, with eight episodes airing weekly through to November 5, and the remaining seven from from January, 2018.

While production continued apace in Toronto, in July members of the cast and the *Discovery* showrunners entertained fans at San Diego Comic-Con 2017, where much was learnt about their characters and the story arc that would play out across the season's 15 episodes. Along with an exhibition of *Discovery* costumes, production stills, concept art, and props, Comic-Con also saw the release of a thrilling new *Discovery* trailer, and there was a real buzz surrounding the show. However, it was at the annual Las Vegas *Star Trek* convention where the sense of anticipation for the new series became truly palpable.

Vegas is where the hardcore *Trek* fanbase assembles every year, and they've been waiting 12 years to see *Star Trek* back on TV. By comparison, the production delays that *Discovery* had faced have been small fry for this dedicated bunch. As excitement mounted over the long weekend, and with just under two months to go until *Discovery*'s scheduled debut, it was clear that *Star Trek* fans were more than ready to embrace it. ⋀

THE WRITER'S ROOM

WHERE DISCOVERY BEGINS

Television doesn't just happen. It takes an army of crewmembers, performers, and artisans to make a success of a show. But without a solid script as a foundation, *Star Trek: Discovery* would be lost in space...
Star Trek Magazine spoke to two members of *Discovery's* Writers Room, Kirsten Beyer and Akiva Goldsman, to uncover what the new *Star Trek* is all about.

Words: Ian Spelling

How ready is Kirsten Beyer for the world to finally see *Discovery*?

"So ready," she says, smiling broadly. "It is so past time, because for me it's been almost a year-and-a-half, which feels like forever. And it's hard to believe, actually, that it's finally almost done and here."

Hoping to get involved with the series, Beyer reached out to executive producer Heather Kadin when the new *Star Trek* was first announced.

"I pitched to Heather," Beyer recalls. "And then it was almost a year later when she told me that, based on that meeting, I was her must-have and that I was going to be joining the staff."

So, what excites Beyer and fellow scribe Akiva Goldsman most about *Discovery*?

"The fact that we're creating a *Star Trek* that is about now," Beyer replies. "Every iteration of this universe lives very much in the time that it was created, and this is such a challenging time to be alive that to be able to filter it through the lens of *Star Trek*, I think, is just personally very helpful for me."

For Akiva Goldsman, it's the process of self-discovery that both the characters and the Federation itself go through during a period of great conflict. Goldsman, who won an Oscar for the screenplay for *A Beautiful Mind*, is on board as a

03

writer and producer, and directed episode three, "Context is for Kings," along with the season finale.

"Sonequa (as Michael Burnham) is a fractal of what is going on with the Federation over the course of the season's arc," Goldsman suggests. "There's all this conversation about conflict vs. no conflict in *Star Trek*, and what the rules are. Obviously, *Star Trek* is full of conflict. It's always been full of conflict. That's half the fun of it. So, what we're doing is pointedly saying we're in a slightly earlier phase of the Federation than the original series, and the notion of these high-minded ideals is tested in the war that provides the context for the first season.

"How do you ensure the survival of the Federation?" Goldsman continues. "What does the Prime Directive (at this point, 'General Order No. 1,') mean? Fundamentally, out of conflict comes reconciliation, comes inclusion, comes coalition, but it doesn't just happen."

PRESERVING THE PRIME TIMELINE

Beyer, well-known to *Star Trek* fans as the author of a dozen *Voyager* novels, is not only on the *Discovery* writing staff, she's also the liaison

04

"We're creating a *Star Trek* that is about now."

KIRSTEN BEYER

between the production team and publishers Pocket Books and IDW. Beyer ensures that the *Discovery* novels and comic books tie-in closely with the series itself, and is very

conscious that some fans are wary of a prequel series treading on the toes of *Star Trek*'s long-established canon.

"You can't let it get into your head about all the ways you could mess it up," she says, addressing worries that both the fans and the writing team share. "Essentially, we know that we've got some room around us, because the previous prequel was set 80 years ago, and the original series isn't happening for another decade. We're taking it as an opportunity, more than something to approach with fear or terror."

Beyer and Goldsman welcome the challenge of surprising audiences, especially through complex characters who might not have enjoyed the spotlight in the earlier series.

"It's a good thing to enter the universe of *Star Trek* through points of view that have previously been unexplored," Beyer notes. "We could give you another captain and a doctor, you know? We could give you all that again, but I find it much more interesting and exciting to see different perspectives."

"I'm really proud of the show," adds Goldsman. "I put my love for *Star Trek* up against almost anyone's, and I think this really is deeply *Star Trek*." ⋀

01 Alex Kurtzman, executive producer of *Star Trek: Discovery*.

02 *Discovery* writer and director Akiva Goldsman, on-stage at *Star Trek Las Vegas*, 2017.

03 Goldsman (second left), with showrunners Aaron Harberts and Gretchen Berg (top right) join the cast of *Discovery* to promote the show during San Diego Comic-Con.

04 *Trek* novelist turned screenwriter Kirsten Beyer on the writers panel at *Star Trek Las Vegas*.

STARFLEET

Protecting the citizens of the Federation, exploring the furthest reaches of deep space. Starfleet vessels, like the *U.S.S Shenzhou* and *U.S.S. Discovery*, are at the vanguard of the Federation's mission, to chart the Galaxy's infinite diversity, and form alliances with new lifeforms and civilizations. The last thing any Starfleet crew wants is to start a war...

FIRST OFFICER
MICHAEL BURNHAM

A human raised as a Vulcan, Michael Burnham faces a choice which could throw the galaxy into chaos.

First Officer Michael Burnham is a child of two worlds: Earth and Vulcan. Born to human parents, she was orphaned at a young age when her family were killed while serving at a Vulcan science outpost. Burnham was taken in by Vulcan Ambassador Sarek and his second wife, the human Amanda, who raised her as their own. Just as Sarek and Amanda became Burnham's surrogate parents, Vulcan became her surrogate home.

Burnham developed a particularly strong bond with Sarek, a revered

> "Burnham developed a particularly strong bond with Sarek, a revered diplomat and master of Vulcan discipline."

diplomat and master of Vulcan discipline. It was at his insistence that Burnham joined Starfleet, having been the first human to graduate from the

Vulcan Science Academy, rather than through the more traditional Starfleet Academy route. Her first assignment was aboard the United Federation of Planets starship the *U.S.S. Shenzhou*, named after a Chinese spacecraft launched in 1999, and she later became first officer under Captain Philippa Georgiou.

Burnham learned and grew under Georgiou, finding a second mother and trusted mentor in her Starfleet captain. She joined the crew of the *U.S.S. Discovery* after serving under Georgiou for seven years. ∧

01

SONEQUA MARTIN-GREEN

02

"*Star Trek's* legacy is one of diversity, and inclusivity. I love that we are taking the next step forward in that legacy, and therefore staying true to it," Sonequa Martin-Green says, describing her character Michael Burnham as "a first contact specialist."

"Being the first black female lead of a *Star Trek* show," she continues, "I don't know if I can put it into words how honored I am, and how blessed I am to be in this position."

Of Burnham's upbringing on Vulcan, Martin-Green says "I become fully indoctrinated with the Vulcan way of life, of seeing the world in this objective, logical way. But what I realize is that my humanity doesn't have to be completely erased, in order for me to embrace everything that I have learned growing up. So it's a very compelling dichotomy that I deal with as Michael."

01 Sonequa Martin-Green as First Officer Michael Burnham.

02 Burnham prepares for a dangerous away team mission, in the *Shenzhou* transporter room.

03 Michael Burnham has questions about her new ship, the *U.S.S. Discovery*.

04 Captain Georgiou (Michelle Yeoh) and Burnham talk tactics.

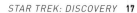

CAPTAIN
GABRIEL LORCA

A brilliant military tactician, Captain Gabriel Lorca must guide the *U.S.S. Discovery* through the turbulent waters of war. But does his steady hand mask another agenda?

Starship commanders must be many things: explorers, scientists, diplomats; but in a time of war a soldier is required. Captain Gabriel Lorca, commander of the *U.S.S. Discovery*, is an officer who exemplifies all those qualities, and more.

Lorca is a complicated individual, whose experience in the fires of the Federation's war against the Klingon Empire has left him with many sharp edges.

> "Lorca's single-minded resolve to end the war makes him the right person to command *Discovery*."

With a hand-picked crew who have placed their trust in his leadership, Lorca's single-minded resolve to end the war makes him the right person to command *Discovery* during this time of conflict. Lorca demands nothing less than the best from his crew, and is particularly adept at bringing maximum effort and ability from those that serve under his command.

But Lorca has depths that are not immediately obvious to those who serve alongside him. An inner turmoil consumes this perfect captain, driving him forward to win the war, by whatever means. ⋀

JASON ISAACS

Jason Isaacs is playing Captain Gabriel Lorca as his own man, rather than referencing Starfleet captains of the past.

"I'm not a captain like any of those people, I would hope," Isaacs says. "If I thought, 'Do I want to be Bill Shatner or Patrick Stewart?' I would have run away crying and hidden in a cupboard. I would do a very poor Picard impression, and an even worse Janeway impression."

Captain Lorca's story, intertwined with that of the *Discovery* and her crew, reflects real-world situations and

stories affecting people across the world today.

"The only point about telling these fantastic stories of the future is to look at ourselves," Isaacs explains. "We live in complicated, troubled times, and those are reflected in our stories and in our characters, and certainly in Lorca.

"You just look for the meat and potatoes, something to act," Isaacs says of Captain Lorca: "He's an interesting and complicated guy, he's a guy damaged by and created by the war that they're in."

SCIENCE OFFICER
LT. SARU

A Kelpien, and the first of his kind to graduate from Starfleet Academy, the ambitious Lt. Saru aspires to his own command.

The Kelpiens are natural born prey, born of an ecosystem where there is no food chain and life is binary – you are either the hunter or the hunted, never both. As a consequence, their biological imperative is to survive in the most unlikely of circumstances. During their early evolution, the Kelpiens developed a keen animal survival instinct, which extends to the protection of others in their care – they can literally sense the coming of death.

Saru enlisted in Starfleet, becoming the first Kelpien to attend

> ## "Saru shares a close, yet competitive bond with Michael Burnham."

Starfleet Academy, and his race's unusual sensory attribute quickly made him a useful officer.

At 6 foot 8 inches tall, Saru is the tallest of the *U.S.S. Discovery*'s crew, but that doesn't mean he's not always looking over his shoulder for

threats. Not to be under-estimated, the Kelpien is always ready to defend himself or his shipmates, using the strength, speed, and power of his gazelle-like legs and hoofed feet.

Saru shares a close, yet competitive bond with Michael Burnham. Their relationship is like that of a brother and sister, often at one another's throats as they try to outdo each other in the eyes of their Starfleet superiors. Both have a long-term ambition to take the captain's seat of their own starship. At the heart of their relationship is deep seated mutual respect, each willing to do their duty and sacrifice themselves for one another if necessary. ⋀

DOUG JONES

"I am a new breed of alien that you've never seen on the shows before, or in the movies," says actor Doug Jones. "This is a whole new thing that we get to discover together."

Saru plays an active role in the Federation's response to the Klingon Empire's aggressive plans for expansion. "The Klingon Empire thinks they are right, "Jones says of

the conflict that drives *Discovery*'s first season. "But in the sensible world of reason, we're trying to peacefully work this out. They won't have it.

"Saru reflects the attitude of Starfleet, that we have to win this, but we must do it in Starfleet fashion" he continues. "We have rules, and we have the Federation's civilized ideals to adhere to."

CAPTAIN
PHILIPPA GEORGIOU

An experienced Starfleet captain, Philippa Georgiou's encounter with an ancient Klingon starship tests her resolve to the limits.

Captain Philippa Georgiou of the *U.S.S. Shenzhou* was Michael Burnham's commanding officer for seven years. Georgiou became something of a second mother and mentor to Burnham over the period they served in Starfleet together, and the two women share both a strong working relationship and a deep personal friendship.

The captain believed her protégé was more than ready for her own command, and wasn't afraid to tell her so, inviting discussion on the subject during one of their final

> "Georgiou is a firm believer in Starfleet's peaceful mission to seek out new life and new civilizations."

missions together. Events would soon tear them apart.

Georgiou is a firm believer in Starfleet's peaceful mission to seek out new life and new civilizations, and find ways to co-exist with each and every one of them. Having experienced the horrors of conflict first hand, Georgiou is particularly dedicated to Starfleet's mission of peaceful exploration and diplomacy. The captain would therefore rather adhere to Starfleet regulations, preferring to hold fire when faced with a potentially hostile force, at least until their intentions have been made clear. That determination is put to the test when Georgiou contacts Starfleet Command with news that her starship has engaged the forces of the Klingon Empire. ⋀

MICHELLE YEOH

02

As Captain Philippa Georgiou, Michelle Yeoh has been enjoying captaining her own starship in *Star Trek: Discovery*.

"The captain's chair is in the most prominent position, and you know whoever sits there commands everyone," she says," adding, "It's a very exciting feeling to be on it."

Yeoh found filming with Klingons intimidating.

"When they emerge, it is quite menacing," the actor reveals. "You take a few steps back and go 'Okay, I don't want to mess with that.'"

However, mess with the Klingons she did and, after one scene went well, Yeoh was moved to show her appreciation to the actor she was peforming alongside.

"One time, I wanted to say thank you and give him a hug," Yeoh says of a close encounter with one Klingon co-performer. It ended up being more painful than congratulatory, as Yeoh had forgotten about his fearsome spiked armor. "Oh my god, ouch," she says.

Asked which of the cast would make the best captain in real life, series lead Sonequa Martin-Green unequivocally chose Yeoh, saying "Everybody is absolutely awesome, but Michelle I would definitely trust the most to be the captain of an actual ship."

01 Michelle Yeoh as Captain Philippa Georgiou.

02 On a desert planet, Georgiou awaits the arrival of her ship, the *U.S.S. Shenzhou.*

03 Yeoh loved her captain's chair on the *Shenzhou* bridge, saying "You know whoever sits there commands everyone."

04 Georgiou beams into a dangerous away mission behind enemy lines.

SCIENCE OFFICER
PAUL STAMETS

For astromycologist Paul Stamets, the primary mission of the *U.S.S. Discovery* is scientific research, not war.

Ask Lt. Paul Stamets about the mission of the *U.S.S. Discovery*, and he's liable to tell you that it was built solely to service his area of expertise: astromycology.

Stamets, an extremely gifted science officer aboard the Federation starship, is an expert in space mushrooms and the vegetative part of a fungus called mycelium. The starship exists, in Stamets' mind at least, for the furtherance of science and the betterment of humanity, and for its Federation allies in the long term. But while his passion for research is one of Stamets' strengths, the ability to form meaningful interpersonal relationships is not. He finds it hard to relate to others he feels are not as intelligent as he is, and at times can be very difficult to be around.

However, Stamets is the sort of person who grows on you. At least that's the experience of his *U.S.S. Discovery* shipmate, and partner, Dr. Hugh Culber. Stamets' relationship with Culber is the exception in his life, rather than the rule, and he knows he's lucky to have found someone willing to put up with his idiosyncrasies. ⋏

ANTHONY RAPP

Actor Anthony Rapp finds it surprising that a franchise on the vanguard of representation has taken so long to to fully reflect society's sexual diversity.

"A little bit of a strange thing in all this time is that there hasn't been an openly gay character as part of it," Rapp says. "So, I'm really honored, and proud, to get to carry that particular flag."

Just as the writers of the original *Star Trek* series didn't overplay the fact that the *U.S.S. Enterprise* had an Asian man and a black woman among its command crew, the writers of *Star Trek: Discovery* don't make a fuss about Stamets' sexuality either.

"The fact of my character's sexual orientation is just one fact among many others, and

is treated as simply and straightforwardly as any other fact of any of the other characters," Rapp confirms.

Of Stamet's dedication to his fungal research, Rapp says, "The stuff that I'm working on in the show is inspired by real science, but it's a very meaningful project that I'm working on."

DOCTOR
HUGH CULBER

Every starship doctor needs patients, and patience – especially if their partner is a scientist with few social skills...

An experienced medical practitioner with a heart of gold, Doctor Hugh Culber draws on his experiences during the Klingon war, and carries a great deal of respect for the soldiers who have come under his care.

Culber reserves his highest admiration for partner Paul Stamets, despite the scientist's often reserved and abrasive manner. Their relationship is very much a case of opposites attract. Sharing their lives while serving aboard a starship in close quarters can be difficult, but the couple are wise enough to ensure their duty to Starfleet is never compromised.

Balancing the requirements of each new mission with the well-being of his patients, Culber is a respected member of *Discovery*'s medical team.

> "Culber reserves his highest admiration for partner Paul Stamets, despite the scientist's often reserved and abrasive manner."

WILSON CRUZ

"As a kid, all I ever wanted to do was be on Broadway and be on *Star Trek*. For me, this is a dream come true, and pretty awesome that I get to share that experience with Anthony Rapp," says Wilson Cruz, who plays one of the *U.S.S. Discovery*'s complement of medical staff, Doctor Hugh Culber.

Culber is the partner of Lt. Paul Stamets, and Cruz hopes that their relationship is a catalyst for viewers who are finding their own identity.

"It's a big deal," says Cruz, "because there is a kid out there who is going to turn on his TV, who is questioning his sexuality or orientation, and they are going to see two men love each other, support each other, and be in awe of each other's genius. And it's not going to be explained – it's just going to be what it is. That kid is going to grow up to know that they can be whatever he or she wants to be. That they are part of the human story."

Despite the chaos of intergalactic war permeating the narrative of *Star Trek: Discovery*, it's the show's characters that truly drive the story.

"The catalyst for the stories is these interpersonal relationships," Cruz confirms. "It's no accident that it's called *Discovery*. The crew are discovering each other, they are discovering themselves."

CADET
SYLVIA TILLY

Fresh from Starfleet Academy, Sylvia Tilly finds herself at the heart of the Klingon-Federation crisis.

If any one member of the *U.S.S. Discovery*'s crew personifies the ship's mission, it would be Cadet Sylvia Tilly. And not unlike the starship aboard which she is serving, Tilly finds herself undertaking her own personal voyage of discovery.

A Starfleet Cadet in her fourth year of study at Starfleet Academy, the United Federation of Planets' main training facility for Starfleet officers, Tilly is enthused by her posting aboard the *Discovery*, and is in a perpetual state of learning.

As a cadet, Tilly has regular contact with senior members of the *Discovery*'s crew as part of her ongoing training. Working closely with Lt. Paul Stamets in the engineering department of the ship, she comes to regard the brusque Science Officer as something of an uncle figure.

As with any starship of the era, space is at a premium aboard the *Discovery*, and many crewmembers share their quarters with a bunk-mate. Tilly is billeted with the ship's Vulcan-raised xenoanthropologist Michael Burnham. Despite their age difference, upbringing, and outlook on life, Tilly and Burnham develop an unlikely friendship. It's a bond which embodies the diversity, understanding and acceptance that the Federation is all about. ⋀

MARY WISEMAN

Actress Mary Wiseman regards Cadet Sylvia Tilly's posting aboard the *U.S.S. Discovery* as something like a stint of work experience during college.

"It's like if you were a journalist, and you had an unpaid internship at *The Times*," Wiseman says. "It's the best possible gig I could have."

Wiseman describes Tilly's state of eager learning, and keenness to absorb new information as "overwhelming" at times, saying "Throughout the season you'll see her find her bearings, and find a real role on the ship."

Wiseman is no stranger to *Star Trek*, having grown up watching *Star Trek: The Next Generation*, and she's no casual fan either. Her favorite episode is the third season story "The Offspring," written by René Echevarria.

"It's the episode when Data had a daughter, named Lal," Wiseman explains. "It's just a gorgeous story about what it means to have a child, and to be a parent."

SECURITY OFFICER
ASH TYLER

U.S.S Discovery security officer Ash Tyler must draw on his inner strength after facing the full horror of the final frontier.

It's fitting that Ash Tyler should serve as the *U.S.S. Discovery's* Security Officer. Tyler already knows what's at stake when a starship's security has been compromised, when its crew has come under threat from a new or familiar foe. He knows, because he's already been on the losing side: Tyler begins his *Discovery* adventure as a Prisoner of War.

Throughout human history, the fate of those taken prisoner by an opposing force during wartime has followed a predictable pattern: torture, for information or the sadistic pleasure of their captors; slavery and hard labor in the cause of the enemy; and the constant threat of death. As their humanity is stripped from them, the prospect of a quick death may seem like a blessed relief.

Aboard the *Discovery*, Tyler's horrific experiences at the hands of his captors motivate him to protect his ship, her captain, and his crewmates from befalling a similar fate. From the relative safety of his new posting, Tyler must deal with the demons he carries from that dark period in his life, and come to terms with how it has changed him as a human being. His affinity with the *Discovery's* captain, Gabriel Lorca, supports Tyler in this ongoing recovery, as does his increasingly close relationship with Michael Burnham. ⌅

SHAZAD LATIF

"He's already dealing with a lot of physical and mental pain that he's gone through," says actor Shazad Latif of Tyler's experiences as a prisoner of war. "So there's a lot to explore there, as he tries to find some normality back on the ship.

"We follow him as he tries to find the sort of man that he is," Latif elaborates,

hinting at the character's twisting story arc. "Tyler is a very complex, painful, and deep character."

While Gene Roddenberry's original *Star Trek* series included a fight scene in every episode, the series' creator insisted that *The Next Generation* stories involved no crew conflict. *Star Trek: Discovery*,

however, approaches storytelling from a very contemporary angle.

"There's so much conflict in this," Latif confirms. "I think that's the only way to have drama. I don't know how they did that before. It's very hard to have no conflict, and I think it will make for a very exciting show."

A GALAXY UNITED

UNDERSTANDING THE UNITED FEDERATION OF PLANETS

The United Federation of Planets was a dream that became a reality, and spread throughout the stars. A galaxy-spanning federal republic that brought races from a thousand worlds together, to exist in peaceful co-existence for the betterment of all.

Words: K. Stoddard Hayes

"FOR WE HAVE AGREED that our worlds hold these truths to be self-evident: that all species are created equal, that their citizens are endowed with certain incontrovertible rights, protected by their societies; that among these rights are life, liberty, and the pursuit of those states-of-being each individual society holds in greatest esteem..."

Excerpt from the Preamble to the Constitution of the Federation

Founded on Earth in 2161, with the signing of the Federation Charter by representatives of Earth, Vulcan, Andoria, and Tellar, the formation of the United Federation of Planets ended a period of mistrust, conflict, and uncertainty that had culminated in a war with the Romulan Star Empire.

The mission of the Earth ship *Enterprise* NX-01, and the diplomatic skill of its captain, Jonathan Archer, were critical to forming the alliances that led to the Federation's formation, ushering in an unprecedented era of peace in the region.

Governance

The Federation's founding documents, the Federation Charter and the Constitution of the Federation, lay out principles of democracy, equality, the rule of law, and peaceful exploration and negotiation. While member races maintain much autonomy in their own territories, their laws must comply in all regards with Federation laws and principles.

The Federation's governing institutions are modeled on many historic democratic governments, of Earth and other planets. They include an Executive branch, headed by an elected President; a legislative branch consisting of a Council of representatives of all member planets; and a judicial branch, led by a Supreme Court.

These branches, and particularly the Executive, have created a large number of specialized agencies devoted to fields such as Archaeology, Science, Cartography, Industrialization, and even such obscure topics as Temporal Investigations. Rumors of secret black ops agencies have persisted since the earliest days of the Federation, despite nearly a century of comprehensive denial by Federation officials.

Starfleet

The Federation's military service, Starfleet is primarily a peacekeeping and exploratory organization, although it incorporates military ranks and discipline, and its ships are armed with state of the art weapons and shielding for defense. Though some Starfleet ships have crews that are predominantly from a single species, officers from many member worlds serve harmoniously together on most ships and installations.

As the Federation's primary means of exploration, Starfleet ships are usually the point of First Contact for unknown species and civilizations. Starfleet officers receive full training in First Contact protocols, including observation of the Prime Directive, particularly for pre-warp societies, and in diplomatic negotiations with species advanced enough to be considered ready for outside contact.

01 The United Federation of Planets has its main headquarters in San Francisco, Earth.

02 The Tellarites and Andorians struck an accord aboard the *Enterprise* NX-01.

03 The Tellarites were one of the founding member-races of the United Federation of Planets.

04 The Klingon Empire remains wary of the Federation's motives, and tensions between the two galactic powers continue to grow.

05 The UFP emblem welcomes visitors arriving at Starfleet Command.

Membership

The Federation has grown rapidly in its first century, with dozens of planetary states as members, and new species constantly seeking admission. The admission process can take several Earth years.

Any planet or planetary nation petitioning for Federation membership must already have a unified democratic government, warp-capable technology, and a society free of oppression or caste-based discrimination. They must also agree to adapt their laws and customs to comply with the Federation's Constitution and laws, and to participate in the many functions of the Federation, including lawmaking, the shared economy, and Starfleet.

The petitioner undergoes a rigorous review process, which can take months or years, with Federation specialists studying every aspect of the society and history of the petitioning member. If the petitioner meets all the criteria of the review, final approval requires a vote by the Federation Council.

Given the large number of sovereign worlds who are already members by the mid-22nd Century,

admitting new members is often politically contentious. Federation members have been known to advocate for approval or rejection of a new member, based solely on their own political or economic interests, rather than the good of the petitioning race or of the entire Federation.

For a potential member with a peaceful and benevolent government, the Federation represents a vast arena of resources for economic, scientific, and cultural exchange. The protection of Starfleet is an important consideration as well, especially for small and vulnerable planets.

04

Enemies

Not everyone loves the Federation, however. The Romulan Star Empire was an adversary of the four founding worlds well before the Charter was signed. Perhaps the biggest irony of recent Romulan history is that the Federation's founding was a direct result of Romulan aggression against these four races. After their defeat in the Earth-Romulan War in 2160, the Romulan Empire retreated within the boundaries of the Neutral Zone, and has refused all outside contact for nearly a century. The Federation can only hope that this watchful peace will continue.

The Klingon Empire has long been hostile to what it perceives as Federation aggression. In the mid-22nd Century, the Empire and its soldiers see Starfleet as their primary adversary, whom they would gladly meet in glorious battle. Klingons are skeptical of the Federation's claims of pacifism and benevolence, believing the Federation has imperial ambitions similar to their own. They also believe that Starfleet practices atrocities they consider dishonorable, such as the torture of prisoners of war.

Starfleet has encountered other planetary states and empires which are hostile because the Federation principles of equality, peace, and the rule of law are a threat to their power and expansion. So far, none have represented as great a threat as the Klingon Empire.

As Starfleet ships push farther out into unknown regions of the Alpha Quadrant, they will no doubt meet many more hostile powers, as well as potential future Federation members. ∧

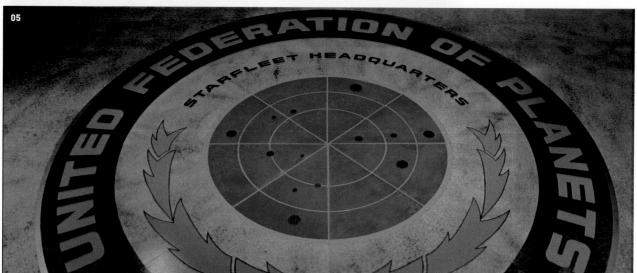

05

VULCAN DIPLOMAT
SAREK

Sarek's cool Vulcan logic could not sway his son, Spock, from enlisting in Starfleet. Can it cope with his surrogate daughter being instrumental in starting a war?

Like most Vulcans, astrophysicist Sarek follows his people's philosophy of suppressing emotions in favor of logic and reason. But his logic is uncertain where his children are concerned. In his role as Vulcan ambassador to the Federation, Sarek married a human, Amanda Grayson, and the marriage produced a son, their Vulcan-human hybrid son, Spock. Later, Sarek and Amanda became surrogate parents to the young human Michael Burnham, after her scientist parents were killed by Klingons.

Sarek assiduously wanted Spock to follow Vulcan ways and teachings,

> "Sarek follows his people's philosophy of suppressing emotions in favor of logic and reason."

in the same way that he had followed the teachings of his own father, Skon, and his grandfather, Solkar. Instead, Spock chose to devote his knowledge to Starfleet instead of the Vulcan

Science Academy. Sarek opposed Spock's enlistment in Starfleet, believing peace should not depend on force, but being neither human nor Vulcan, Spock felt at home nowhere else.

Sarek's relationship with Michael Burnham was different. His mentorship of the human girl would lead her to embrace Vulcan logic, and attend both the Vulcan Learning Center and the Vulcan Science Academy, before accepting a commission in Starfleet, at Sarek's behest. Sarek watched her rise through the ranks to become the *U.S.S. Shenzhou*'s first officer. ⋀

01

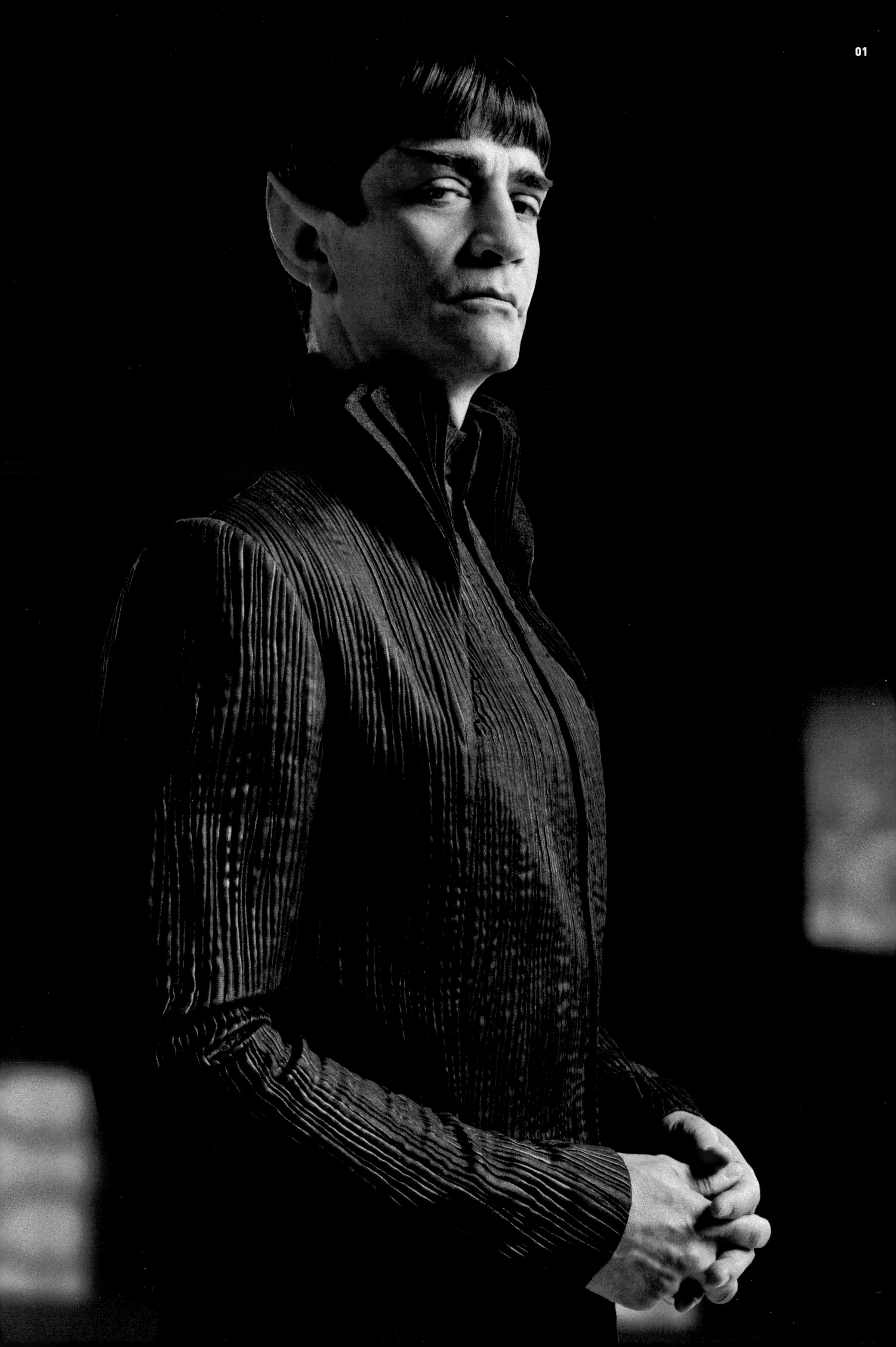

JAMES FRAIN

Actor James Frain is relishing playing a younger version of Sarek, Spock's father from the original *Star Trek* series, in *Star Trek: Discovery*.

"One of the things that was always fascinating was the fact that he married a human, and that's Spock's back story," says Frain. "He's a mentor to Michael Burnham, so it's interesting that he has a fully human child too."

Frain finds Sarek "endlessly fascinating, and complex, and ambivalent."

"Vulcans still have emotions," he adds, "And there's a real struggle that goes on with that, because he's brought a human into his life, so now he has a half-human child and a fully human child. This is very challenging to him. It opens up a door that he didn't know was there."

02

01 James Frain as Sarek.

02-04 Designed by Gersha Phillips, and fabricated in Toronto by *Star Trek: Discovery*'s costume department, Sarek's traditional robes reflect the Vulcan culture and its devotion to a life of pure logic, serious intellectual pursuits, and spiritual contemplation.

03

04

GALACTIC ENTREPRENEUR

HARCOURT FENTON MUDD

Flamboyant civilian trader "Harry" Mudd is a man with an equally flamboyant reputation. And it isn't necessarily a good one.

Harcourt Fenton Mudd would describe himself as an interplanetary businessman, merely embracing the trading opportunities afforded to him by the United Federation of Planets. But many of those that do business with Mudd (known as Harry to friends and enemies alike) consider him to be little more than a dangerous conman.

Outwardly flamboyant, Mudd's ebullient nature masks a darker, more dangerous side, which comes to the

> "Mudd's ebullient nature masks a darker, more dangerous side, which comes to the fore when his profit margin is under threat."

fore when his profit margin is under threat. His modus operandi is to gain the trust of his victims (he'd prefer to call them "customers") until they believe in whatever dubious contraband he's pushing, and then see how much profit he can wrangle out of them.

Mudd is the last man in the galaxy to be bothered with rules and regulations. From love drugs to false patents, counterfeit intellectual property to robot wives, Mudd always has a plethora of deals on the go. He'd happily sell anything to anyone, or anyone to anything. ⋀

RAINN WILSON

02

Actor Rainn Wilson feels blessed to have been cast as Harry Mudd in *Star Trek: Discovery.*

"I got to fire a phaser. I got to be transported in the transporter room. I got to sit in the captain's chair," Wilson says, enthusiastically.

"These things that, when I was five, six, seven, eight, ten years old, watching the original *Star Trek* series, and when I was in my twenties watching *The Next Generation*, are just icons of Western culture. And I got to participate. It just blew my mind beyond my wildest dreams."

Wilson says that his take on Mudd, played by Roger C. Carmel in original series episodes "Mudd's Women" and "I, Mudd," is an iconic character, reimagined.

"I got to take what Roger Carmel did with the original character and then add my own, special sauce. He created a fantastic, flamboyant, over-the-top, mischievous but kind of dangerous character. I get to bring a little bit more to it."

01 Rainn Wilson as Harcourt "Harry" Fenton Mudd.

02 Designed by Gersha Phillips, and built by the *Star Trek: Discovery* costume team, Mudd's outfit is cut primarily from leather.

03 Mudd's outfit was inspired by the stage costumes of 1980s pop star Adam Ant.

04 The costume was displayed in an exhibition at San Diego Comic-Con in 2017.

05 First played by Roger C. Carmel, Harry Mudd has the distinction of being the only guest character on the original *Star Trek* to be featured in two episodes.

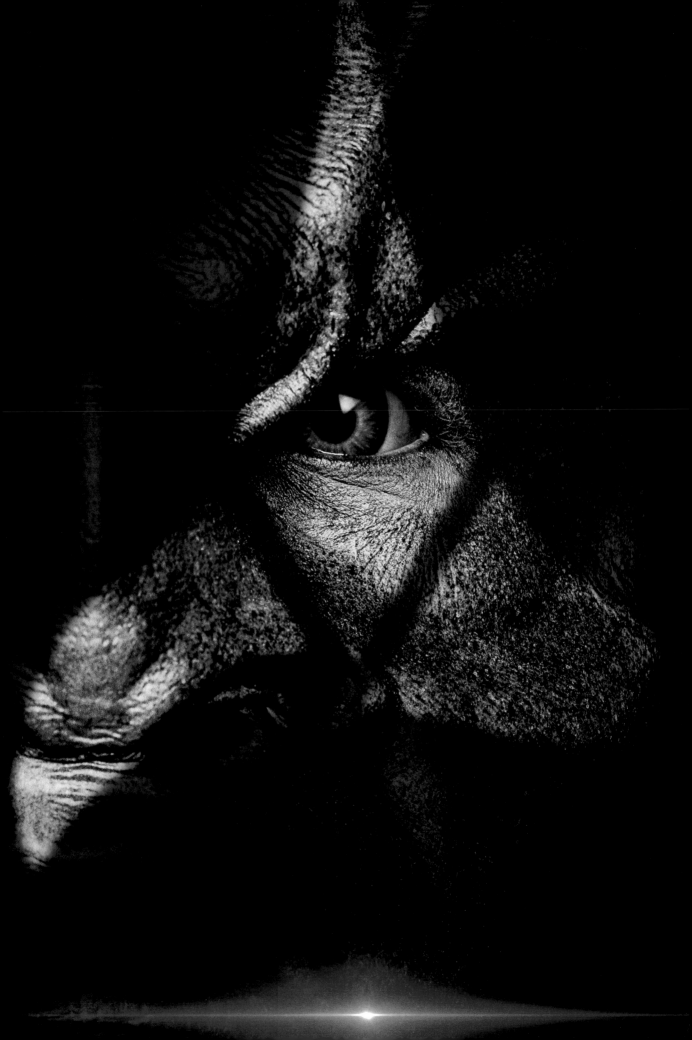

THE KLINGON EMPIRE

Established on Qo'noS by Kahless the Unforgettable, the Klingon Empire conquered its way across the Beta Quadrant, becoming the dominant force in the region. Yet by the 23rd Century the Empire was in disarray, its Great Houses mired in internecine squabbles over honor and doctrine, until T'Kuvma resolved to unite the houses against the United Federation of Planets.

COMMANDER
KOL

An ambitious warrior of the House of Kor, Commander Kol is hungry for power.

One of the Great Houses of the Klingon Empire, the House of Kor is a powerful and respected voice among the Empire's 24 most prominent houses. Under the leadership of respected military leader Kor, son of Rynar, the royal blood of the Klingon Imperial family burns fiercely in the veins of its warriors.

Kol regards the honor of his family as paramount, and would sooner die than live with a mark on the name of his ancestral lineage. For

> "Kol harbors ambitions of his own, and embraces the opportunities offered to him by war."

him, the House is everything, and every member is responsible for the actions of their kin.

And yet, Kol harbors ambitions of his own, and embraces the opportunities offered to him by war with the Federation. While Kol may be proud of his heritage, and a dogged defender of the House of Kor, everything that he does is in support of the honor and increasing power of Kol himself.

Kol has no love for the Federation, and humans especially, seeing any overture they make towards peace as an attempt to rob the Klingon people of their identity. ⋀

KENNETH MITHCELL

"When I auditioned, I didn't know I was auditioning to be a Klingon," says actor Kenneth Mitchell, who spends his days on set buried beneath the complex prosthetics of Kol. "I tell my kids, 'I'm going to be a Klingon,' and they're like 'What is that?'"

Mitchell's children may be too young to recognize the word Klingon, but they would be even harder pressed to recognize their own father when fully made-up as Kol.

"It takes three-and-a-half hours to get into the make-up!" reveals the actor, who spends those hours in

the make-up chair running over his lines, to better deliver the complex vocalizations that the Klingon language requires.

"It's an incredibly challenging and complex language. It's complicated for a reason, so that it feels alien-like," Mitchell adds. "It takes a lot of muscle memory to memorize every separate syllable. My kids and my family think I'm crazy, but at the end of the day, it is all worth it. It adds such an amazing texture to the show, and is a real asset to helping the audience learn more about the Klingon culture."

BATTLE DECK COMMANDER L'RELL

A child of two Klingon houses, where do the allegiances of battle deck commander L'Rell truly lie?

A respected warrior and battle deck commander, L'Rell is a key player in the ongoing war between the Klingon Empire and the Federation, and of a conflict within the Empire itself.

Unusually within the strict honor codes of Klingon society, L'Rell belongs to two houses. Her mother was of the House Mokai, while her father was of

> "L'Rell feels that serving two houses is an advantage that others do not fully appreciate."

the House Girjah, whose leader is keen to unite all the Klingon houses following generations of disarray within the Empire. Her ties to both houses effect how she is viewed by some Klingons, but L'Rell feels that serving two houses is an advantage that others do not fully appreciate.

The distinctive white armor of the battle deck commander marks L'Rell out as worthy of respect. ⅄

MARY CHIEFFO

The re-imagined look of the Klingons in *Star Trek: Discovery* goes far deeper than a simple redesign for contemporary audiences, as Mary Chieffo explains.

"There's a whole reasoning behind it," she says. " I really, deeply believe we are in line with what has come before, but with a new kind of nuance.

"With the compassion that we are giving to the Klingons," Chieffo adds, "you really get a window into who we are, and our humanity, or our 'Klingon-anity!"

L'Rell's ancestry, and her relationship with the two Klingon houses she belongs to, are a big part of the character's story arc.

"The exploration of houses is really fun," continues Chieffo. "L'Rell's relationship with the

Klingon Empire, and with the Federation – who I am to Kol is different to who I am to the Federation – there's a very

interesting difference in opinion on exactly how to go about affecting change. And you're going to see that on both sides."

Discovery will see its Klingon characters speaking their own language with English subtitles. Chieffo has worked hard to learn the alien tongue, but regrets that she's not yet fluent.

"We are dedicated to the language," Chieffo insists. "It makes sense, if we speak to each other, we would speak in our native tongue. With Klingon, every word is unfamiliar. We don't take it lightly, making sure every word is pronounced correctly. We know we want to be able to really dive into what's happening between L'Rell and Kol, and not just be overwhelmed with the Klingon."

'WE ARE KLINGONS'

A BEGINNER'S GUIDE

"Today is a good day to die."
Such is the mantra of the Klingon warrior, foot soldiers of the Klingon Empire. As the United Federation of Planets stands on the brink of war with this complex foe, an understanding of their history, society, and beliefs has never been more necessary.

Words: Chris Gardner

PHYSIOLOGY

The average Klingon warrior is slightly taller and heavier than an average human, and the warrior caste is open to both males and females (although it is sometimes difficult for non-Klingons to distinguish between the two sexes).

Klingon society is built on an ancient house system, with every Klingon being a member of one of the many family-based houses. There are 24 "Great Houses" in the hierarchy of Klingon society, and their representatives populate the High Council.

The distinctiveness of each family line is reflected in the traditional armor that defines each house, and again in preferred styles of personal grooming. The Empire is so vast that Klingons from one house might appear quite different from a Klingon born at the opposite edge of Klingon space.

> The larger-than-life exploits of Kahless have become legendary, making it hard to separate fact from fiction.

Outwardly different from humans due to bony cranial and spinal ridges, internally the Klingons benefit from multiple redundant organs. This redundancy is called *brak'lul*, and means that, in any given fight, a Klingon warrior is usually the last being left standing. For example, Klingons have two livers, where humans have only one, and their hearts have eight-chambers, compared to the four chambers of a human heart. With 23 ribs to crack, and only 12 in a human, it is clear that a Klingon's robust frame will outlast even the most highly-trained human combatant.

KAHLESS THE UNFORGETTABLE

The Klingon Empire was founded a millennium ago by legendary warrior Kahless the Unforgettable, after he killed his tyrannical rival, Molor. It was Kahless who first united the Klingon people, and introduced their concept of honor and the laws relating to it.

The larger-than-life exploits of Kahless have become legendary, making it hard to separate fact from fiction, and songs are sung about his many exploits throughout the Empire. How much is true, and how much is embellished, is uncertain, but these tall tales and epic songs fuel an Empire. Kahless is an ever-present figure in Klingon daily life.

By all accounts, Kahless was as great a lover as he was a warrior, and his Lady Lukara was beside him when he defended the Great Hall of Qam-Chee against 500 of Molor's warriors.

02

It was here that Kahless wielded the first *bat'leth*, proposing to Lukara after the battle was won.

Kahless wielded his legendary *bat'leth*, known as the Sword of Kahless, at the Battle of Three Turn Bridge, where he is said to have defeated an entire army single-handedly. It was a useful tool, used for many a diverse task. With it, Kahless is said to have skinned the Serpent of Xol, harvested his father's field, and carved a statue of his beloved Lukara. The legendary Fek'lhr, a feral Klingon beast said to torture dishonored

Klingons in the afterlife, is also said to have fallen to the sword of Kahless.

Klingon warriors believe there is power in the name Kahless, and they turn to him daily in ceremonial mid-day prayer, offering up requests for the souls of their family's dead warriors, and the souls of honorable friends. Ahead of battles, warriors also call upon Kahless to guide their generals and starship commanders on the battlefield.

With the spirit of Kahless the Unforgettable as their ally, the Imperial Klingon fleet and its horde of

warriors are an interstellar force to be reckoned with.

DEATH AND HONOR

Honor is at the heart of Klingon life and death, with every good Klingon aspiring to live by the way of the warrior code. If necessary, they are prepared to die in defending those high principles.

Kahless, Klingon warriors believe, meets the souls of honorable warriors in the Klingon afterlife, which is known as *Sto-Vo-Kor*. No warrior fears death, but all Klingons

01 Klingons warriors perform the death howl, warning the honored dead that a Klingon warrior is arriving.

Klingons do not bury their dead. They treat the body as an empty shell to be discarded.

Unlike other cultures, Klingons do not bury their dead. They treat the body as an empty shell to be discarded.

Legend tells of how Kahless journeyed to the afterlife and rescued his brother from the Barge of the Dead, an ancient ship that plies the kos'Karri serpent-infested river of blood to Gre'thor.

FIRST CONTACT

First Contact between the Klingon Empire and Earth was a mistake that led to the early launch of the United Earth Starfleet's first Warp 5 capable starship, *Enterprise* NX-01, on April 1, 2151.

A Klingon scout ship crash-landed near the Moore family corn farm on the outskirts of the American city of Broken Bow, Oklahoma, and the *Enterprise's* maiden voyage became a trip to Qo'noS to return its pilot home.

Klaang, the pilot of the crashed Klingon vessel, was on a secret mission for the High Council of the Klingon Empire, and was being pursued by a pair of Suliban soldiers when his ship made its crash-landing on Earth. Klaang had discovered that the Suliban Cabal was plotting the downfall of the Klingon Empire by setting the Great Houses against one another. The Klingon had collected evidence and encoded it in his body's DNA, so that only those who knew where to look could find it.

After escaping his ship, Klaang, an ever-resourceful warrior with the heart of Kahless the Unforgettable, lured the Suliban soldiers into a grain silo which he then destroyed with his handheld disruptor weapon. The Klingon warrior was then seriously injured after being shot by a member of the Moore family, who had come to investigate the disturbance armed with a plasma rifle.

Klaang was cared for at United Earth Starfleet Medical in San Francisco by the Denobulan doctor Phlox, a specialist in alien physiologies, before it was decided by Starfleet Command to return Klaang to Qo'noS.

It was an eventful journey, both for Klaang and the crew of the *Enterprise*, but their mission to return Klaang to his people was, eventually, successful. This mission made the NX-01's captain, Jonathan Archer, and communications officer, Hoshi Sato, among the first humans to set foot on the Klingon homeworld. Human visitors to Qo'noS would not become a regular occurrence, as cultural misunderstandings led to the straining of Klingon-human relations.

Two years later, Captain Archer was sentenced to life imprisonment at the Klingon Empire's penal colony on the frozen asteroid of Rura Penthe, for harboring fugitives of the Empire aboard the *Enterprise*. The Empire held Archer to account at a tribunal hearing on the Klingon colony world of Narendra III, where he was found guilty of conspiring against the Empire.

The Empire transported Archer to Rura Penthe, known as "the aliens' graveyard," because any alien who ended up doing hard labor in the colony's dilithium mines seldom lasted a year before dying from overwork, malnourishment, or exposure to the cold.

The Empire's relations with Starfleet were strained still further when Archer was broken out of Rura Penthe by the *Enterprise's* armory officer, Lt. Malcolm Reed.

EPIDEMIC

There are some things that the Klingon Empire would rather not remember.

In an effort to emulate the work of a rogue human scientist, Dr. Arik Soong, Klingon scientists hoped to create genetically augmented Klingon warriors, using enhanced human DNA left over from Earth's Eugenics wars.

Klingon doctor Antaak, a specialist in metagenic research, worked on the project at the Qu'Vat Colony. But as Klingon genetic material was being combined with Soong's augmented human DNA, it became inadvertently compromised with a flu virus, quickly becoming a plague that threatened to cause the Empire's extinction.

The plague caused humanification of infected Klingons, causing their cranial ridges to disappear, and their foreheads to become as smooth as a human's. The plague was seen as a great dishonor, and its effects felt in Klingon society for decades thereafter. Now, Klingon leader T'Kuvma is determined to reassert the purity of Klingon identity. ⚑

fear dying a dishonorable death, and being condemned to spend eternity on the Barge of the Dead. The barge is fabled to be piloted by the first Klingon, Kortar, who destroyed the Klingon gods because they were too much trouble. Kortar was condemned to remain on the barge as eternal punishment for this misdeed.

Upon the death of a friend or family member, Klingons will gather around the body, lift their heads to the heavens, and howl. The Klingon death ritual is said to warn the dead that a Klingon warrior is about to arrive.

PREPARED FOR BATTLE

THE KLINGON ARMORY

A warrior race, for whom every weapon is imbued with the honorable victories of a thousand ancestors, the Klingon armory of *Star Trek: Discovery* adds intricate layers of symbolism and detail to iconic designs from *Star Trek*'s past.

Working alongside Glenn Hetrick at their Los Angeles-based Alchemy Studios, Neville Page was tasked with creating the signature look for *Star Trek: Discovery*'s Klingons. But this was not their first brush with *Star Trek*'s most recognizable antagonists.

Although a sequence shot for J.J. Abrams' *Star Trek (2009)* ended up on the cutting room floor, Page was able to try something new with the warrior race for *Star Trek Into Darkness*.

"J.J. said, 'What are we going to do with them?' So I thought, 'No offense to previous Klingons, but can we make them sexy?'" reveals Page. "That was my personal ambition – let's make them as tough, as warrior-like as possible, but as beautiful, powerful beings.'"

That idea has been carried through to *Discovery*, from the exaggerated, almost sculptural ridges of the Klingon's faces, to the intricately detailed armor that suggests a deep connection with tradition and a complex culture. Page was excited about the opportunity to create something iconic, especially with the Torchbearer armor.

"I really wanted to take advantage of the opportunity to do something that you just can't do normally," says Page. "It's because of the technology, primarily. You can't hand-sculpt those shapes, symmetrically, within the time and money. I thought, 'This is a really great opportunity to do something that's so visually complex and appropriate.'"

THE TORCHBEARER

Chosen through a sacred ritual, the Torchbearer exists for one task alone – to activate an ancient obelisk that will sound The Call to unite all the Klingon houses.

Worn only by the Klingon warrior chosen to serve as the Torchbearer, this symbolic battle armor is also a sophisticated EV space suit.

BEHIND-THE-SCENES

The armor and weaponry of *Discovery*'s Klingons have embraced and augmented cultural notes from *Star Trek's* original Klingons, employing a mixture of Middle Eastern, Mongolian, and Byzantine influences to achieve the Klingon aesthetic. The ornate, ceremonial blades located on the boots of the Torchbearer's suit are reimagined versions of Klingon weapons from *Star Trek: The Next Generation*, and the *Star Trek* movies and television series.

Built by Glenn Hetrick and Neville Page's Alchemy Studios in Los Angeles, cutting edge 3D printing techniques were employed in the creation of the Torchbearer, using 100 individual components from Neville Page's digital designs.

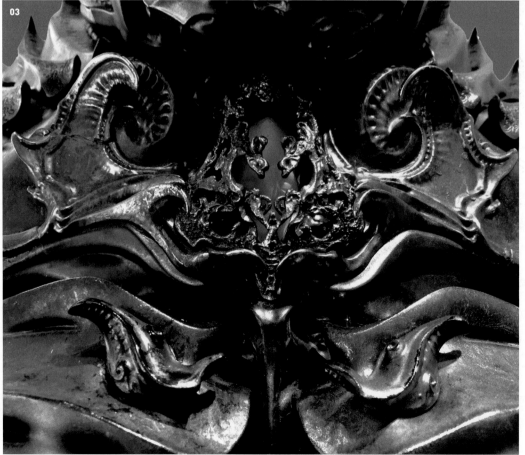

01 The Torchbearer armor used 100 individual components, 3D printed from digital models.

02 The familiar symbol of the Klingon Empire adorns the Torchbearer's shoulder pauldron.

03 Ornate detailing, such as on the Torchbearer's chest plate, was made possible by 3D printing technology.

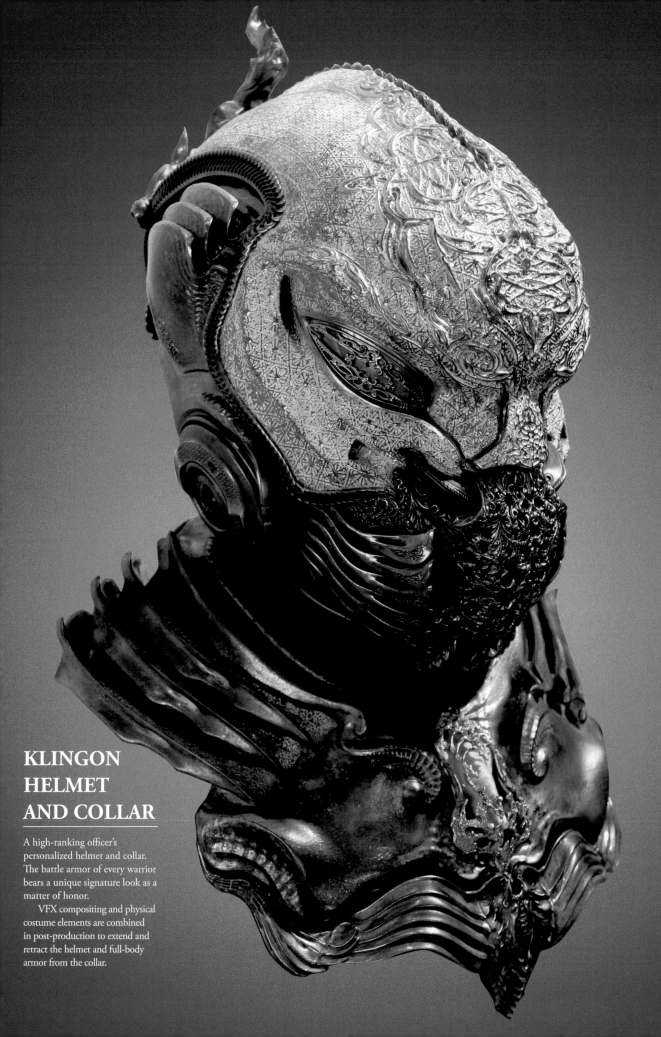

KLINGON
HELMET
AND COLLAR

A high-ranking officer's personalized helmet and collar. The battle armor of every warrior bears a unique signature look as a matter of honor.

VFX compositing and physical costume elements are combined in post-production to extend and retract the helmet and full-body armor from the collar.

WEAPONS

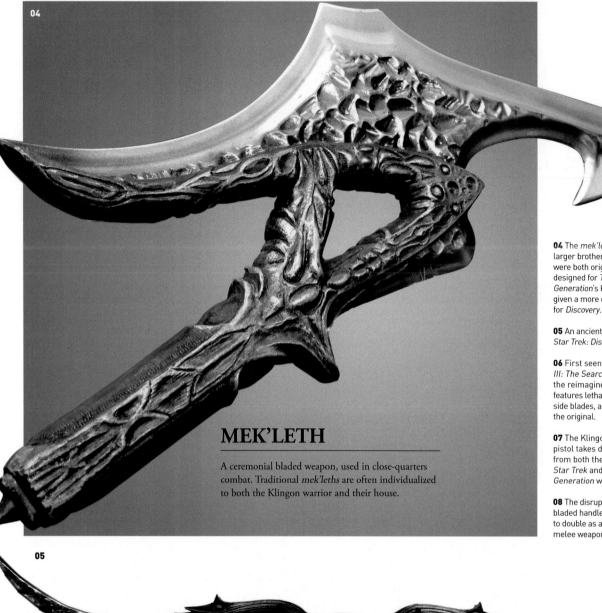

04

04 The *mek'leth*, and its larger brother the *bat'leth*, were both originally designed for *The Next Generation*'s Klingons, and given a more detailed look for *Discovery*.

05 An ancient *bat'leth* from *Star Trek: Discovery*.

06 First seen in *Star Trek III: The Search for Spock*, the reimagined *d'k tahg* features lethal extendable side blades, as did the original.

07 The Klingon disruptor pistol takes design cues from both the original *Star Trek* and *The Next Generation* weapons.

08 The disruptor rifle has a bladed handle that allows it to double as a deadly melee weapon.

MEK'LETH

A ceremonial bladed weapon, used in close-quarters combat. Traditional *mek'leths* are often individualized to both the Klingon warrior and their house.

05

BAT'LETH

The preferred weapon of the Klingon warrior, the *bat'leth* and *mek'leth* props were hand-sculpted from high-density foam, before being 3D scanned. The resultant 3D model was then refined, and machine-milled from aluminum. The surface of the blades were hand-carved from a poured resin, while the handles were hand-carved from foam and then cast in rubber.

06

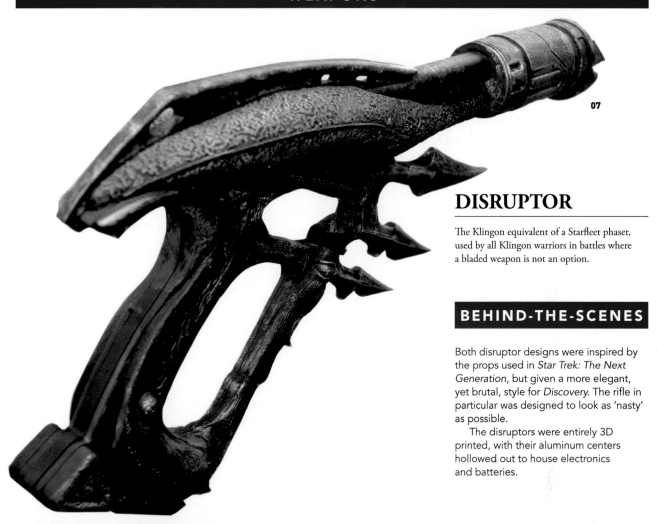

07

DISRUPTOR

The Klingon equivalent of a Starfleet phaser, used by all Klingon warriors in battles where a bladed weapon is not an option.

BEHIND-THE-SCENES

Both disruptor designs were inspired by the props used in *Star Trek: The Next Generation*, but given a more elegant, yet brutal, style for *Discovery*. The rifle in particular was designed to look as 'nasty' as possible.

The disruptors were entirely 3D printed, with their aluminum centers hollowed out to house electronics and batteries.

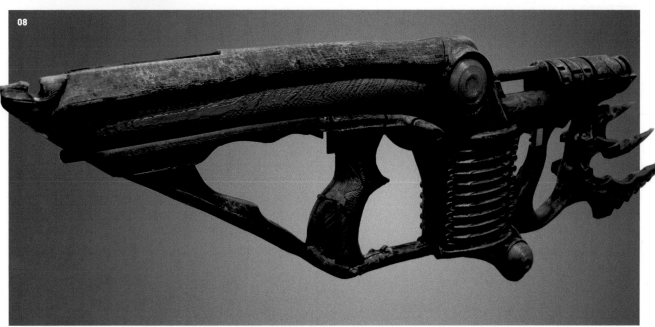

08

T'KUVMA

T'Kuvma (played by Chris Obi) seeks to unite the 24 great Klingon houses and halt the encroachment of others across the Empire's borders. His elaborate clothing honors ancient Klingon ways, and the path of honor set forth by Kahless the Unforgettable.

BEHIND-THE-SCENES

Designed by Gersha Phillips and Suttirat Anne Larlarb, T'Kuvma's ornate costume is comprised of two prime layers: a tunic and a chest plate. The tunic is made up of three types of leather, with task and hydraulic tubing to form panels that mold into a skirt. The intricate chest plate is made up of 3D-printed beads, with a magnetic back closure that creates a seamless appearance. The design incorporates claw-like Swarovski crystals, and vintage lace around the collar.

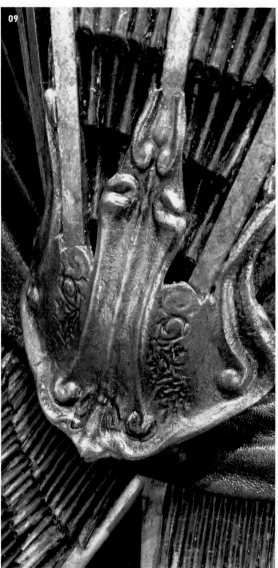

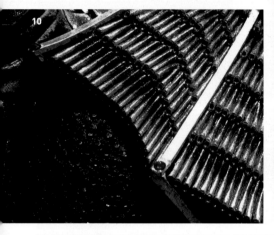

09 T'Kuvma's rank and importance is shown through the impressive decoration on his armor, including this buckle.

10 Crimson Swarovski crystals on T'Kuvma's collar and chest plate add a hint of blood-red danger to the costume.

11 The armor worn by warriors of the House of T'Kuvma follows the same angular style as his, but with less ornamentation.

12 The Klingon leader T'Kuvma (played by Chris Obi), is determined to unite his race against the Federation.

HOUSE OF T'KUVMA ARMOR

The gray armor favored by warriors of the House of T'Kuvma follows ancient Klingon designs, paying tribute to their ancestors and to the path of honor walked by Kahless.

BEHIND-THE-SCENES

Designed by Gersha Phillips and Suttirat Anne Larlarb, both male and female warrior armor was constructed piece-by-piece, with individually stained, hand-pressed leathers that were painted and molded for texture. The complex costumes took a team of 10 costumers an estimated 110 hours to create.

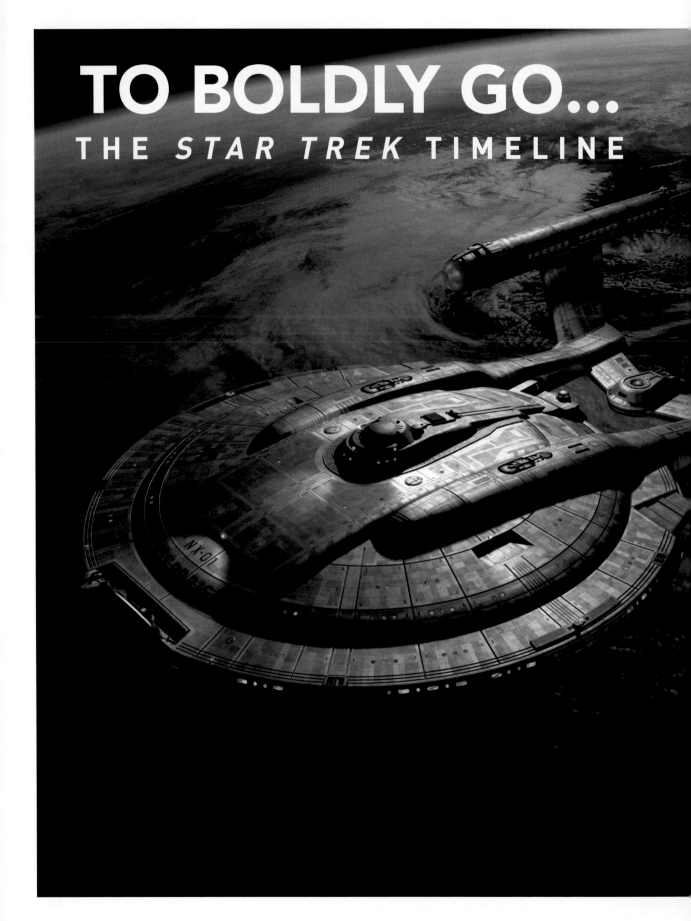

TO BOLDLY GO...
THE *STAR TREK* TIMELINE

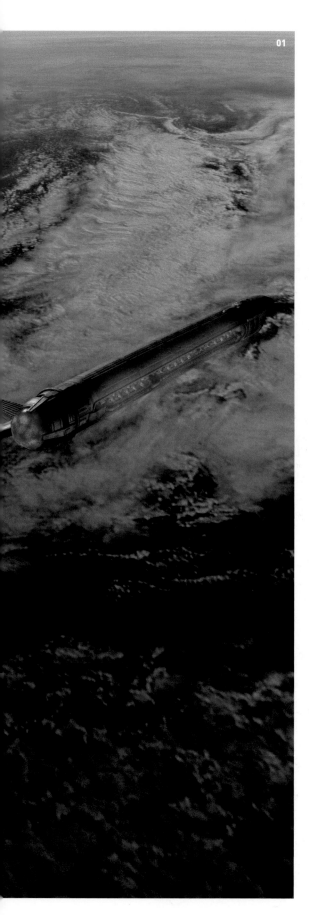

01

Star Trek, first broadcast in 1966, has been thrilling sci-fi fans for over half-a-century. *Discovery* brings the franchise full circle, in a story that unfolds a decade before the adventures of Captain Kirk and his valiant crew.

Set midway through the 23rd Century, the original *Star Trek* explored strange new worlds from the perspective of its own turbulent era, reflecting the huge social changes of the 1960s in the tales it told of humankind's future. The subsequent *Trek* television sequels – *The Next Generation*, *Deep Space Nine*, *Voyager*, and prequel series *Enterprise* – continued to make sense of our world through science-fiction allegory across the decades.

As *Discovery* takes us back to the 23rd Century on a new adventure, here's where it fits within *Star Trek*'s future timeline.

2063

Zefram Cochrane, the inventor of the warp drive, conducts his first test flight, prompting the Vulcans to initiate first contact with Earth.

2151

When *Star Trek: Enterprise* begins, the success of the Warp 5 program has placed Captain Jonathan Archer on the cusp of the unknown, in charge of a small crew of 83, aboard a ship that is as untested as its personnel. Like the settlers of the American West, the first *Enterprise* crew is breaking ground on a bumpy road towards technological advancement and interspecies harmony.

Earth launches the *Enterprise* NX-01 following its first encounter with a member of the Klingon race, Klaang, who was shot by a farmer after crash landing in a field in Oklahoma. Archer's first mission is to safely return Klaang to his home world, a mission complicated by interference from Suliban intruders, and a mysterious figure fighting a Temporal Cold War! With Vulcan science officer T'Pol, and down-to-Earth engineer Trip Tucker at Archer's side, it's the perfect set-up for the adventures to come.

As the first prequel in *Star Trek*'s timeline, the show's focus was to flesh out events that had previously only been mentioned on-screen, as it aimed to bridge the gap between our real-world history and the original *Star Trek* series by exploring the many firsts of a maiden voyage at warp speed.

2161

10 years after the initial launch of the *Enterprise*, Earth prepares to join an alliance that will eventually lead to the founding of the United Federation of Planets.

As a television series, *Enterprise* ended after four seasons, and the series finale featured *The Next Generation*'s Commanders William Riker and Deanna Troi, looking back at the heroic contribution of the NX-01's crew to the galaxy's history, via the magic of a Holodeck simulation. The episode ended a continuous, 18-year run of new *Star Trek* episodes on television.

2254

Nearly 100 years later, and Captain Christopher Pike is in command of Starfleet's flagship, the *U.S.S. Enterprise* NCC-1701 (in *Star Trek*'s pilot episode, "The Cage"). A distress signal beckons Pike and his crew, including Vulcan science officer Spock, to the surface of Talos IV. But the crew discovers its a trap set by a telepathic race called the Talosians, who want to capture Pike for breeding purposes.

Ultimately, Pike refuses to submit to the fantasies the Talosians generate from his memories, because he prefers reality – however harsh. His first officer's willingness to sacrifice herself and the crew, rather than allow the aliens to enslave them, convinces the Talosians that humans are simply too violent and dangerous to keep around.

"The Cage" clearly illustrates how series creator Gene Roddenberry wanted the show to explore morality,

02

03

01 The *Enterprise* NX-01, Earth's first warp 5-capable ship.

02 Under the command of Captain Jonathan Archer, the crew of the first Starfleet vessel named *Enterprise* made a unique contribution to galactic peace.

03 Captain Kirk and his first officer, Mr. Spock.

04 The *U.S.S. Enterprise*, following her refit at the end of her historic 5-year mission.

05 Kirk and his closely-knit command crew, in their later years of service.

06 Captain Jean-Luc Picard takes command of a new *Enterprise*, in 2364.

psychology, and humanity. However, the network was worried by the cerebral nature of the pilot, and ordered a second pilot to be made. In the more action-packed, though equally thought-provoking "Where No Man Has Gone Before," time had shifted some years ahead, and now Captain James T. Kirk commanded the *Enterprise*.

2255

Taking place 10 years prior to the storied voyages of Captain Kirk, *Star Trek: Discovery* is a prequel to the original *Star Trek*'s five-year mission. This new installment in the timeline promises to explore a narrative gap in the Federation's history which has previously been untapped.

The first season features a clash with the Klingon Empire, and pays homage to the original series by bringing back characters including charismatic conman Harry Mudd, and Spock's father, Sarek. The future Vulcan ambassador intriguingly links Spock with *Discovery*'s new protagonist, Michael Burnham. As Spock's adoptive sister, Burnham faces similar issues of self-identity to those which bubbled beneath his logical exterior in the original series and movies.

2265

With Captain Kirk at the helm, the *U.S.S. Enterprise* NCC-1701 embarks on a five-year mission of exploration, diplomacy, and discovery. With a record-setting number of first contacts (and perhaps thrown punches), a brash attitude toward protocol that

sometimes leads him to flout the Prime Directive, and an affinity for trusting his gut and charming the ladies, Kirk stands out as a captain like no other. With Mr. Spock and the impassioned Dr. Leonard McCoy at his side, the trio became an unstoppable force, with Spock's rationality and McCoy's humanism a perfect counterpoint to Kirk's gut-instinct feistiness.

Add a diverse crew that included African communications officer Uhura, Asian helmsman Sulu, and Russian navigator Chekov (a big deal for a show that aired during the height of America's cold war with the Soviet Union), *Star Trek* marked itself out as something different, something unique. Its stories held powerful messages about compassion, civility, and the very emotional and moral bonds that make us human.

2269

Serving as a continuation of the *U.S.S. Enterprise*'s five-year mission, the two-dimensional adventures of *Star Trek: The Animated Series* were often far from simplistic, making big sci-fi ideas accessible to a new, younger audience.

2273–2293

Over the course of six feature films (*Star Trek: The Motion Picture, Star Trek II: The Wrath of Khan, Star Trek III: The Search for Spock, Star Trek IV: The Voyage Home, Star Trek V: The Final Frontier,* and *Star Trek VI: The Undiscovered Country*), twenty years of in-universe history unfolded. Old foes like the vengeful Khan, new and angrier Klingons, and stuck-in-the-past Starfleet Admirals threw the original crew back together, as they protected Earth and the entire Federation from numerous threats.

What's more, as the much-loved cast aged alongside their characters, new perspectives were added to *Star Trek*'s exploration of the human condition.

2364

Flash forward to nearly a century later, and a new *Enterprise* and her exploits are our case studies for *Star Trek: The Next Generation*.

Under the leadership of Captain Jean-Luc Picard, the *U.S.S. Enterprise* NCC-1701-D continues to seek out new life and civilizations, with stories that took a deeper and often more nuanced look at the complex social issues facing the crew.

Picard ushered in a more refined age, and not just because of his French ancestry or his penchant for Earl Grey tea. By this point in Federation history, bigotry and sexism have been all-but been eradicated, and the stories placed a greater emphasis on individual characters and their lives beyond their duties aboard ship.

The series also offered characterization that heightened the importance of each individual member of the crew.

By placing the empathic Deanna Troi in a seat on the bridge next to the captain, the show signaled the deep importance of sympathy and emotional understanding in this period. Diversity among Starfleet officers found new meaning in Mr. Worf, a Klingon raised by humans, and in the android Data who, unlike Spock, wanted to become more human.

07

07 *Deep Space 9*'s crew and their allies defended the Alpha Quadrant from the invading Dominion.

08 The *Intrepid*-class *U.S.S. Voyager* became the first Starfleet ship to navigate the Delta Quadrant.

09 *Voyager*'s diverse crew consisted of many races, including humans, Vulcans, Bajorans, a Talaxian, a former Borg, and a holographic doctor.

New adventures called for new enemies, so we met the likes of the Ferengi, the Cardassians, and most notably the nefarious Borg, a bio-mechanical collective which sought to absorb any species or technology that it encountered, in a quest for perfection. Then there was the mischievous Q, a recurring, god-like pest of a being, with the power to twist reality, or fling Picard's ship directly into the Borg's path.

2369

In a departure from the exploratory thrust of its predecessors, *Star Trek: Deep Space Nine* saw Commander Benjamin Sisko reluctantly take charge of a remote space station outpost, on the far reaches of Federation space.

The scenario was again a variation on the Wild West theme – a frontier town on the edge of civilization – but *DS9* delivered a darker, more difficult look at Federation life. With plots largely tethered to the station, the crew often felt more like a family, with all the related interpersonal drama that entails.

Sisko, too, was arguably more complex than the captains that came before. The harrowing loss of his wife, the trials of raising a son alone, and the challenges of overseeing *Deep Space 9* may have shaped his character, but the Dominion War defined it. For the first time, Starfleet wasn't simply guarding the peace and forging new bonds, it was helping the Federation defend its very ideals from dictatorial invaders, the Dominion. Through the crisis of war, Sisko's moral compass was tested, and ethical gray areas examined, in stories where it was not only acceptable but necessary to do the wrong thing for all the right reasons.

2371

With the even-keeled Captain Kathryn Janeway taking charge, the *U.S.S. Voyager* was designed to return to Starfleet's founding principles of scientific exploration, and take *Star Trek* back to its space-faring roots.

On its maiden voyage, the ship was swept 70,000 light years away by an omniscient alien array, and stranded

in the Delta Quadrant, where the crew faced a staggering 75-year journey home. With a crew composed of Starfleet officers, renegade Maquis, a holographic Doctor and, later, an orphaned Borg drone, the long journey bound the characters together, as grudges, bigoted beliefs, and stereotypes were stripped away. They weren't just exploring the galaxy, they were fighting to survive.

Janeway was the first female lead to grace the franchise, and made for a formidable but compassionate captain. By bringing exploration back to the fore, and imbuing the journey with the urgency of a stranded ship, lost and alone, the classic formula was reinvigorated through this magnificent glimpse at perseverance despite impossible odds.

2371-2379

Graduating from television, *The Next Generation* replaced the original crew for *Star Trek*'s next four movie outings. But before they took full control of the helm, there was one final opportunity for Captain Kirk to shine.

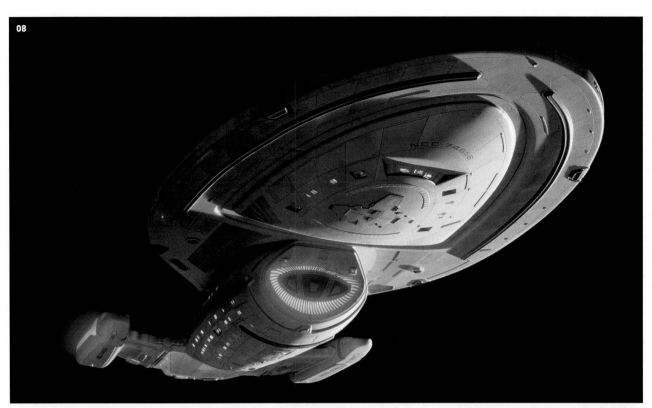

10 Captain James T. Kirk died in heroic circumstances, much as he'd lived, in 2371.

11 Picard's *Enterprise*-D crew were on-hand to witness Earth's first contact with the Vulcans.

Kirk's appearance in *Star Trek Generations* cemented the feeling of the old guard making way for the new, with a plot that connected the two crews through a dangerous refugee and a mysterious energy ribbon, and which killed Kirk off in the final reel.

Three additional feature films saw Captain Picard and his cohorts undertake new missions, but the cinematic draw of *Star Trek* was beginning to wane. In *Star Trek: First Contact*, the crew pursued the Borg through time to 2063, where they witnessed Zefram Cochrane's historic warp speed achievement; they discovered the fountain of youth in *Star Trek: Insurrection;* and, thanks to diminishing box-office returns, saved the universe one final time in *Star Trek Nemesis.*

2387

Ambassador Spock saves the entire galaxy from a supernova by creating a quantum singularity, which not only absorbs the exploding star but accidentally destroys the planet Romulus in the process. A Romulan mining ship, the *Narada*, and Spock's craft are also sucked into the singularity, reemerging in the past to completely alter the course of *Star Trek* history as we know it...

2233

The future came full circle when J.J. Abrams delivered a perfect blend of time-traveling antics, alternate timelines, and some almost-familiar faces, in the movie *Star Trek (2009)*. The new feature film reboot neatly side-stepped *Star Trek*'s in-universe canon by employing a plot device that shifted the action into a reality just to the left of the classic series, recasting the characters from the original television show with fresh, new faces. It also injected a jolt of new life into the franchise.

The Romulan mining ship *Narada* emerges through the back end of Spock's red matter-induced singularity, in the year 2233. Its commander, Nero, is hell-bent on revenge, and attacks the *U.S.S. Kelvin* – aboard which one George Kirk serves. In his 12 minutes as captain of the Starfleet vessel, George sacrifices himself and the ship in an effort to save 800 lives, including those of his wife and newborn son – James T. Kirk.

2258

By the time the singularity ejects Spock into a new reality created by the *Kelvin* Incident, the year is 2258. In this alternate timeline, younger versions of Kirk, Spock, McCoy, Uhura, Sulu, and Chekov must come together to save Captain Christopher Pike and the Earth from Nero's anarchy.

Star Trek was reborn, and further adventures *Star Trek Into Darkness*, and *Star Trek Beyond* continued to rewrite Federation history in a reality that sits comfortably alongside the Prime timeline, where the *Kelvin* incident never even happened... ⋀

DEFINING *STAR TREK*

Star Trek's utopian vision of the future, where Earth is not only at peace, but serving as the capital of a United Federation of Planets, has always centered around a core group of characters, a crew of Starfleet officers who would become a family.

The original crew was envisioned by the show's creator, Gene Roddenberry, as being diverse in gender, race, and species; equal, respected, and served with a solid moral compass when making first contact with new life and previously undiscovered civilizations. Whenever a new crew has assumed their mantle, the characters and adventures have maintained a connectivity to Roddenberry's egalitarian vision.

At the most basic level, *Star Trek* is a story about the family you choose to surround you, the choices you make that define you, and the boundless ingenuity and heart it requires to keep on going. It's a celebration of diplomacy, compassion, and overcoming seemingly insurmountable odds.

Above all, *Star Trek* asserts that the human journey is just beginning.

12 In an alternate timeline, Federation history followed a different path, although its values of peaceful co-existence remained true.

STARFLEET ISSUE

ICONIC DESIGNS REIMAGINED

With more than a nod to the iconic designs of the original *Star Trek* television series, the futuristic kit issued to the Starfleet personnel of *Star Trek: Discovery* combines familiar outlines with a contemporary spin.

Using cutting-edge prop-making technology, the challenge facing *Discovery*'s designers was how to strike a balance between a design aesthetic, established half-a-century ago, and props that meet the demands of a modern television audience, while maintaining an in-universe sense of continuity.

HAND PHASER

Invented during the 23rd Century, and utilized primarily for defense, the first phasers are a space-age Swiss Army knife of sorts; wielded as an energy-beam-firing weapon, as a cutting tool for on-the-fly repairs, or even as an energy source. In a pinch, a phaser can even heat up rocks, helping a stranded crewman to survive in sub-zero temperatures.

The Type-2 Phaser pistol emits a focused energy beam with eight adjustable settings, from stunning a target to complete disintegration. It also incorporates a detachable, palm-sized miniature version, the Type-1 phaser, for easier concealment during clandestine undercover work and diplomatic missions.

Prop builders for the original *Star Trek* series were inspired by the cutting-edge technology of their own time, with a remote control made by electronics company Magnavox providing an early basis for the phaser's shape.

Matt Jefferies and brother John were the designers that defined *Star Trek*'s iconic look, with props master Wah Chang bringing their concepts to life. For the phaser, John sketched out half a dozen concepts, from which Matt and Gene Roddenberry hand-selected elements that would be incorporated into the final phaser prop. Wah Chang later modified the paint scheme, at Roddenberry's request, for greater visual impact on screen.

The new phaser for *Discovery* takes several cues from the Type-2, with a playful nod towards its in-universe predecessor, the laser pistol. The prop was given a 'tougher' look to indicate a more militaristic functionality, which echoes the Phase-pistols seen in *Enterprise*. Built and painted in Los Angeles, each phaser is 3D-printed, with a removable magazine that houses batteries and electronics.

01 The original series pilot episode "The Cage" featured a laser pistol with a rotating barrel, and a muzzle featuring three emitters. This design element was incorporated into the new *Discovery* phasers.

02 The type 2 phaser pistol, as used throughout the original *Star Trek* series, featured an adjustable beam and detachable type 1 phaser unit.

03 Tricorders have always been one of *Star Trek*'s trademark devices, used by medics, scientists, and engineers to scan everything from the geology of a rock to the health of a tribble.

TRICORDER

Whether in sick bay or on the surface of a strange new world, the tricorder is an invaluable tool for Starfleet scientists, enabling them to collect, analyze, and record data during missions. The tricorder is, in effect, a tiny laboratory that produces results at lightning speed.

Used across departments, from science and medical, to operations and engineering, these sleek, black and silver handheld devices are a ubiquitous sight aboard Starfleet vessels. Featuring three distinct segments – display and controls, a compartment for data chips, and a slot for a detachable sensor – they are a vital element of any away team's arsenal of equipment.

As with the communicator props, the new tricorders provide their data readouts, via a loop of animated video footage on a miniature LED screen. Constructed and painted in Los Angeles, the tricorder is entirely 3D-printed, and includes a removable handheld scanner, much like the originals. The design also borrows from versions seen in the *Star Trek* films *The Search for Spock*, and *The Final Frontier*.

From the beginning, Gene Roddenberry had an idea that the tricorder design could be a potential money-spinner. With its strap reminiscent of a handbag or purse, and several women on the show utilizing the device, he'd hoped it might become a popular toy for girls.

Roddenberry was also keenly aware that the imagined technology of his futuristic enterprise could one day become our reality. That vision moved a step closer to reality in 2017, when Final Frontier Medical Devices and Dynamical Biomarkers Group were both announced as winners of the Qualcom Tricorder XPRIZE to invent such a device.

PHASER PULSE RIFLE

With styling that clearly places it in the same armory as the phaser pistol, the pulse rifle was inspired by Pup rifle designs of today. Observant fans will notice that the design pays tribute to previous props, lifting influences from the original series and *Star Trek: Enterprise*.

The copper filament chambers inside the barrel mid-section is a deliberate nod to an original series prop: Kirk's phaser rifle in "Where No Man Has Gone Before," while the weapon's silhouette echoes that of the particle rifles used by MACO troops in *Star Trek: Enterprise*.

04 In *Star Trek*'s second pilot episode, "Where No Man Has Gone Before," Captain Kirk armed himself with a distinctive phaser rifle, which the *Discovery* phaser pulse rifle references.

04

05 The mesh grille on the front of the communicator has a dual purpose. When closed it protects the device's controls, and when flipped open it becomes a sensitive antenna.

06 An original series communicator in use. *Discovery*'s version of the device is very close to the original prop in size and design, but features a modern LED screen and 3D printed parts.

07 The communicator from *Star Trek*'s first pilot episode "The Cage."

COMMUNICATORS

Standard issue for away missions, the communicator provides a vital connection between a crewmember and their ship. A flick of the wrist opens the device's cover with an electronic chirp, notifying the user that a channel has been opened, and enabling them to patch into the communications system aboard ship.

Used to relay information, send a distress signal, or request a transport, the communicator can transcend its primary function to become a tool or a weapon – a sonic disruption from two communicators linked together is powerful enough to cause a rockslide.

The earliest 23rd-Century communicators were more akin to pocket-sized radios, with a clear casing exposing the electronics inside, and a protective mesh screen that doubled as an antenna. As technology moved forwards, the device retained the mesh screen cover, but became smaller and far more streamlined.

05

Wah Chang's chunky communicator design for *Star Trek*'s pilot episode, "The Cage," was completely overhauled for the series. Two new operational props and eight dummy versions were originally constructed, costing around $1,000 in design and production costs. The props often fell victim to the force of an actor's overzealous wrist action, their hinges breaking as the mesh cover snapped backwards.

The *Discovery* communicator is heavily influenced by the communicators from the original *Star Trek*, and is made from milled aluminum, although numerous details have been tweaked and updated. The rotating moire pattern that signified an open communications channel on the original prop was powered by a wind-up stopwatch. For the modern version, this has been replaced by a sophisticated, animated display screen, provided by a smartphone that sits inside the casing. The mesh cover bears a strong resemblance to that seen on the communicators from the movie, *Star Trek II: The Wrath of Khan*.

06

07

THE TRANSPORTER

By the 23rd Century, the near instantaneous subspace teleportation of multiple living individuals has become standard practice, and an essential element of a Starfleet ship's exploration capability. With an engineering expert at the controls, the transporter platform converts the very molecules of a person into raw energy, which is then beamed to another location and converted back into matter, reassembling the molecules into their exact original pattern.

Early transporter technology was unreliable at best – intended to more easily move inanimate objects, not people – and met with skepticism that ranged from safety concerns to metaphysical debates over how such a machine might alter biological beings. Even as the technology was perfected, natural events like a rogue ion storm could disrupt a transporter signal, causing drastic consequences. However, such events are rare.

08 Captain Georgiou and first officer Burnham prepare to transport.

09 The *U.S.S. Shenzhou* transporter room. The operators are protected behind the control console's screen.

STARFLEET UNIFORMS

Star Trek: Discovery costume designer Gersha Phillips and her Toronto-based team went to extraordinary lengths to bring new layers of texture and complexity to the show's outfits, and this extended to the new-look Starfleet uniforms.

FABRIC

Specialist fabrics were sourced for *Discovery*'s incredible costumes from all over the world, including the use of bespoke, 3D-printed and acid-etched fabrics. The cloth used for the main Starfleet duty uniforms, for example, came from Switzerland, where it was dyed in a custom navy blue shade.

DESIGN

The two-piece duty uniforms consist of separate tunic and pants, but the overall blue design and detailing echoes the all-in-one outfits used throughout the four seasons of *Star Trek: Enterprise*, even down to zipper-fastened pockets in the pants.

This design choice suggests an evolution in uniforms, mixing the utilitarian look of *Enterprise* with the primary colors of the original *Star Trek* series, which are reflected in the metallic gold, copper, and silver detailing of the new uniforms.

STARFLEET DUTY UNIFORM

COMMAND DIVISION

Personnel in the command division wear a two-piece duty uniform featuring gold side compression panels and detailing. A ribbed, navy blue panel stretches across both shoulders.

01 Compression panels on the side of the uniform feature a flexible fabric incorporating the Starfleet emblem.

02 Captain Georgiou's uniform. Note the added gold detailing across the shoulders and four rank-identifying pips on the Starfleet badge.

SCIENCES

The standard duty uniform for officers in
Starfleet's sciences division features silver
detailing. Worn by Lieutenant Commander
Saru (Doug Jones) on the *U.S.S. Shenzhou*
and Lieutenant Paul Stamets (Anthony Rapp)
aboard the *U.S.S. Discovery*.

MEDICAL

Medical officers wear 'hospital white' variants
of Starfleet sciences division uniforms. The
silver side compression panels and delta
shield pattern signifies medical's place within
the sciences division, but are marked by a
distinctive badge insignia.

OPERATIONS

This variant duty uniform features elbow-length
sleeves and alternate detailing. The copper side
compression panels and delta shield pattern
signifies an officer in Starfleet's operations
division, which encapsulates ship operations,
security, and engineering functions.

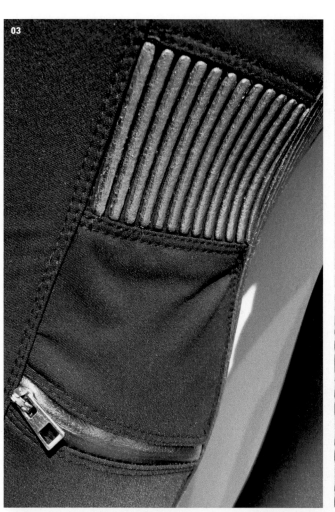

03 A variant duty uniform worn by Starfleet officers features elbow-length sleeves and alternate detailing.

04 Medical officers wear 'hospital white' variants of Starfleet sciences division uniforms.

05 The variant operations division uniform.

06

STARFLEET TACTICAL JUMPSUIT & VEST

For missions beyond the safety of a starship, specialized variations on standard issue uniforms offer additional protection and equipment.

Starfleet officers engaged in combat situations or potentially hazardous away missions are issued an armored tactical vest and distinctive version of the duty uniform, trading metallic accents for a low-profile navy blue compression panel. Flashlights are installed in the shoulders of the vests for guidance. Vests also contain additional functional elements for attaching specialized mission gear.

06 For missions beyond the safety of a starship, specialized variations on standard issue uniforms offer additional protection and equipment.

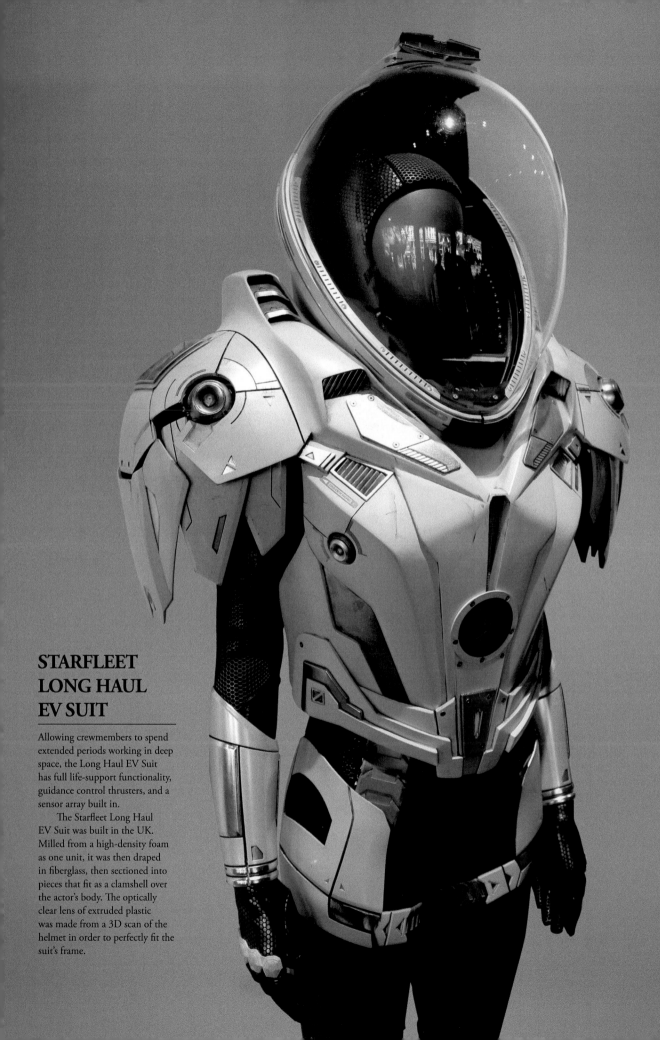

STARFLEET LONG HAUL EV SUIT

Allowing crewmembers to spend extended periods working in deep space, the Long Haul EV Suit has full life-support functionality, guidance control thrusters, and a sensor array built in.

The Starfleet Long Haul EV Suit was built in the UK. Milled from a high-density foam as one unit, it was then draped in fiberglass, then sectioned into pieces that fit as a clamshell over the actor's body. The optically clear lens of extruded plastic was made from a 3D scan of the helmet in order to perfectly fit the suit's frame.

STARFLEET INSIGNIA BADGES

The color of the Starfleet emblem badges matches the trim of the uniforms. Each Starfleet division can be identified by the trim color, in much the same way as the color of the tunics in earlier *Star Trek* series marked out the role of a crewmember (red for security, for example).

GOLD
COMMAND

SILVER
SCIENCES AND MEDICAL

COPPER
OPERATIONS

BEHIND-THE-SCENES

Created in Toronto by *Discovery*'s art department, wax models of the badges were created from 3D prints. Plaster molds were then made, into which silicon bronze was poured. The badges were then plated in the three custom *Discovery* colors and polished by a specialist jeweler.

THE ART OF
DISCOVERY
CONCEPTUALIZING THE FINAL FRONTIER

01

01 This concept illustration of the *U.S.S. Discovery* by John Eaves includes a concave, thick-edged saucer section.

02

03

02 "Crepuscular A8"
Costume designed by
Gersha Phillips.

03 (Insert) Concept art:
Burnham and Captain
Georgiou explore a
desert planet.

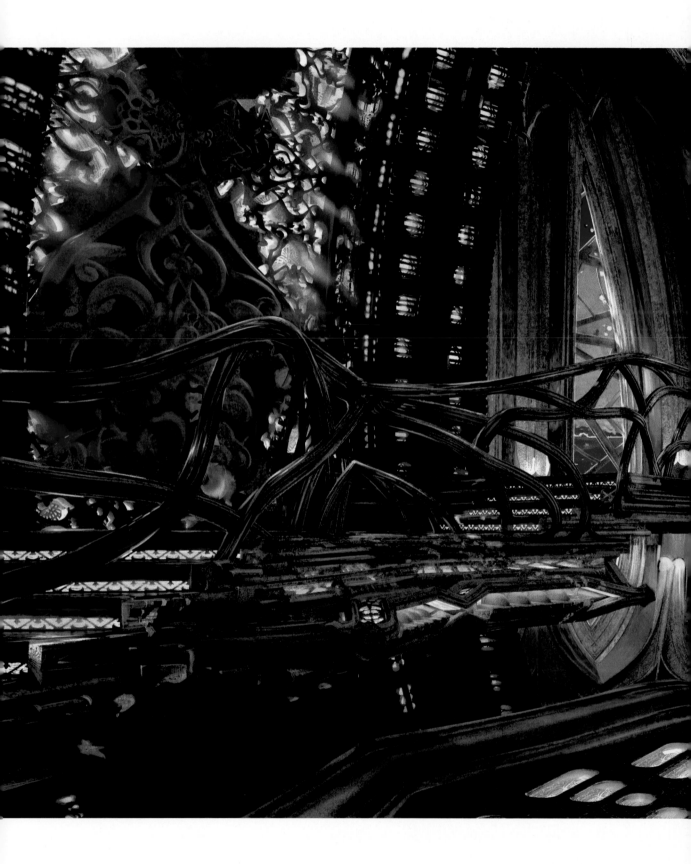

04 A work-in-progress concept rendering of
the Klingon Sarcophagus ship's bridge (aft view).

04

05 Concept drawings of the *U.S.S. Shenzhou* (belly and top views).
The ship's look was being refined into early 2017. Note the bridge
section on the underside of the primary saucer.

06 Concept art: The *U.S.S. Shenzhou* faces
off against T'Kuvma's Klingon forces.

07

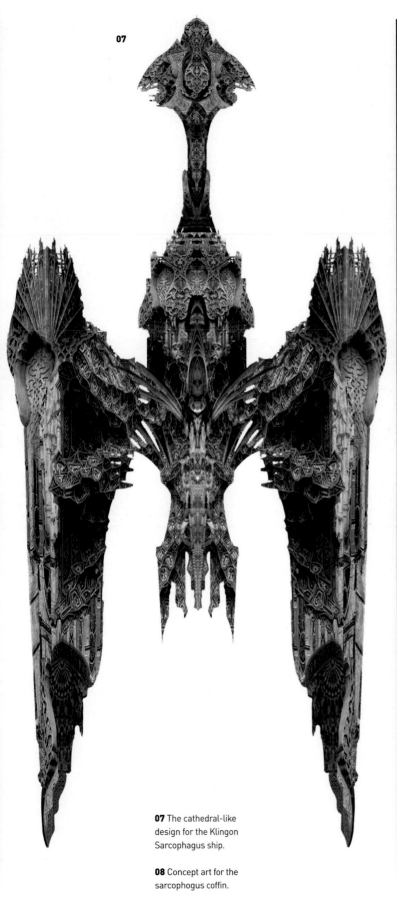

08

07 The cathedral-like design for the Klingon Sarcophagus ship.

08 Concept art for the sarcophogus coffin.

OTHER GREAT TIE-IN COMPANIONS FROM TITAN
ON SALE NOW!

Rogue One - The Official Mission Debrief
ISBN 9781785861581

Rogue One - The Official Collector's Edition
ISBN 9781785861574

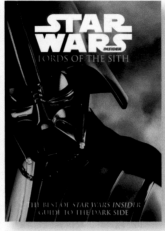

Star Wars: Lords of the Sith
ISBN 9781785851919

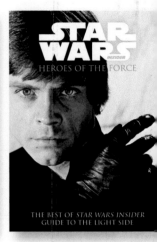

Star Wars: Heroes of the Force
ISBN 9781785851926

The Best of Star Wars Insider Volume 1
ISBN 9781785851162

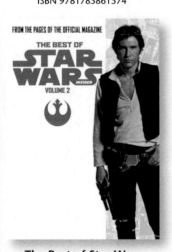

The Best of Star Wars Insider Volume 2
ISBN 9781785851179

The Best of Star Wars Insider Volume 3
ISBN 9781785851896

The Best of Star Wars Insider Volume 4
ISBN 9781785851902

Star Trek: The Movies
ISBN 9781785855924

Fifty Years of Star Trek
ISBN 9781785855931

Star Trek - A Next Generation Companion
ISBN 9781785855948

Alien Covenant: The Official Collector's Edition
ISBN 9781785861925

TITANCOMICS
For more information visit www.titan-comics.com